KIERKEGAARD: A GUIDE FOR THE PERPLEXED

For

THE GUIDES FOR THE PERPLEXED SERIES

Levinas: A Guide for the Perplexed, Benjamin Hutchens

Adorno: A Guide for the Perplexed, Alex Thomson

Deleuze: A Guide for the Perplexed, Claire Colebrook

Wittgenstein: A Guide for the Perplexed, Mark Addis

Husserl: A Guide for the Perplexed, Matheson Russell

Quine: A Guide for the Perplexed, Gary Kemp

Merleau-Ponty: A Guide for the Perplexed, Eric Matthews

Sartre: A Guide for the Perplexed, Gary Cox

Gadamer: A Guide for the Perplexed, Chris Lawn

KIERKEGAARD: A GUIDE FOR THE PERPLEXED

CLARE CARLISLE

continuum

Continuum International Publishing Group
The Tower Building
11 York Road
London SE1 7NX

80 Maiden Lane
Suite 704
New York, NY 10038

British Library Cataloguing-in-Publication Data
A catalogue record for this book is available from the British Library.

ISBN 0 8264 8610 X (hardback) ISBN 0 8264 8611 8 (paperback)

Library of Congress Cataloging-in-Publication Data
A catalog record for this book is available from the Library of Congress.

Typeset by Servis Filmsetting Ltd, Manchester
Printed and bound in Great Britain by
Cromwell Press Ltd, Trowbridge, Wiltshire

CONTENTS

Acknowledgements   vii

List of Kierkegaard's Works   viii

Introduction   1

1 Kierkegaard's Life and Works   6
   Kierkegaard: a brief biography   6
   Parallels between Kierkegaard's life and philosophy 14
   Who is the 'real' Kierkegaard?   22

2 The Question of Communication   25
   Indirect communication   25
   Kierkegaard's pseudonyms   33
   Writing against philosophy   39

3 Kierkegaard's Critique of Hegel   45
   Hegel's philosophy: rationalism, history,
   reconciliation   45
   Hegelian philosophy in Denmark   52
   Either/Or: Kierkegaard's critique of Hegel   56

4 Subjectivity and Truth   63
   Concluding Unscientific Postscript: the truth of
   Christianity   63
   The aesthetic, the ethical and the religious   75
   Kierkegaard's spheres of existence   83

5 The Problem of Sin   90
   What is sin?   90
   The Concept of Anxiety: the psychology of sin   94
   The Sickness Unto Death: sin and despair   101

90-110   136 - 146

CONTENTS

6 *Fear and Trembling*: Faith Beyond Reason   110
   Introducing the story of Abraham   110
   Responding to suffering: resignation and faith   117
   Abraham and ethics – three problems   124

7 *Philosophical Fragments*: The Paradox of Christianity   132
   Socrates, Hegel and Christianity   132
   Climacus's paradox: how can truth be learnt?   136
   Faith and history   146

Conclusion   153

Further Reading   158

References   161

Index   164

ACKNOWLEDGEMENTS

Most of this book was written in the Kierkegaard Library at St Olaf College in Northfield, Minnesota, where I spent a month as a visiting scholar in the autumn of 2005, and I am indebted to the Kierkegaard Foundation and the Leverhulme Trust for funding this work. I would like to thank Gordon Marino and Cynthia Lund for welcoming me to the Library and for making it such a peaceful, comfortable place to work in; thanks also to the other Kierkegaard scholars, particularly Leo Stan and Roy Sellars. I am very grateful to Elizabeth Galbraith of the Department of Religion at St Olaf for her generous help and friendship, and to Sharon Gates-Hull for providing me with a home and family during my stay in Northfield. I am grateful too for my brief but truly inspiring encounter with Jonathan Lear, whose visit to St Olaf happily coincided with my own.

Daniel Wilson, Don Cupitt, Neale Scantlebury and Leo Stan read the first draft of the book, and their comments have been invaluable. I also want to thank Nigel Warburton and Hugh Pyper for their advice early on, and Mike Weston for suggesting that I write this book.

And thank you to Josh for reminding me to keep it real, and to Don Cupitt and George Pattison for so many great conversations about Kierkegaard.

LIST OF KIERKEGAARD'S WORKS

Early writings

1834   *Another Defense of Woman's Great Abilities*
1838   *From the Papers of One Still Living*
1841   *The Concept of Irony with Continual Reference to Socrates*

Pseudonymous works

1843   *Either/Or*, edited by Victor Eremita
        Fear and Trembling, by Johannes de silentio
        Repetition, by Constantin Constantius
1844   *Philosophical Fragments*, by Johannes Climacus
        The Concept of Anxiety, by Vigilius Haufniensis
        Prefaces, by Nicolaus Notabene
1846   *Concluding Unscientific Postscript*, by Johannes Climacus
        Stages on Life's Way, edited by Hilarius Bookbinder
1849   *The Sickness Unto Death*, by Anti-Climacus
1850   *Practice in Christianity*, by Anti-Climacus, edited by S. Kierkegaard

Religious discourses

1843–5 *Eighteen Upbuilding Discourses*
1845   *Three Discourses on Imagined Occasions*
1847   *Upbuilding Discourses in Various Spirits*
        Works of Love
1848   *Christian Discourses*
1849   *The Lily of the Field, The Bird of the Air: Three Devotional Discourses*
        Three Discourses At The Communion On Fridays: The

*High Priest, The Publican, and The Woman Who Was a
Sinner*
1850　*An Upbuilding Discourse*
1851　*Two Discourses At The Communion On Fridays*
1855　*The Changelessness of God*

Other signed works
1846　*Two Ages: A Literary Review*
1848　*The Crisis and a Crisis in the Life of an Actress*
1849　*Two Minor Ethical–Religious Essays*
1851　*On My Work as An Author*
　　　For Self-Examination: Recommended in the Present Age
1855　*This Must Be Said – So Let It Be Said*
　　　The Moment
　　　What Christ Judges of Official Christianity

Writings published posthumously
Johannes Climacus, or De omnibus dubitandum est (1842–3)
The Book On Adler / On Authority and Revelation (1846–7)
The Single Individual (1846–7)
The Point of View for My Work as an Author (1848)
*Armed Neutrality, or My Position as a Christian Author in
　　Christendom* (1848–9)
Judge For Yourself! (1851)
Journals and Papers

For my father

INTRODUCTION

The nineteenth-century Danish philosopher Søren Kierkegaard was one of the most gifted, creative, and provocative thinkers within the Western philosophical tradition. His books challenge and inspire readers to think differently – not only about human existence in general, but about their own lives. Kierkegaard suggests that philosophy should concern itself not with abstract theories, but with those questions that confront every existing individual: how should I use my freedom? how can I respond to suffering? how can I be true to myself, or to another person? how do I live a meaningful, worthwhile life? Unlike most of his predecessors, he insists that the most important aspect of a human being is not reason, but passion. Kierkegaard's penetrating, uncompromising analysis of the human condition marks the beginning of a new direction in philosophy: he is known as the father of the 'existentialist' tradition, which shaped the intellectual life of Europe throughout the twentieth century, and he had an enormous influence on philosophers such as Heidegger, Sartre and Wittgenstein.

But Kierkegaard would have been reluctant to call himself a philosopher. In fact, he was scathing about contemporary philosophers' attempts to translate the depth and complexity of human existence into a set of abstract concepts, put together to form a rational system. Above all, Kierkegaard is a religious writer, and his main concern is the truth of Christianity. For him, this does not mean establishing the truth of Christian doctrine, but figuring out how to become a true Christian – how to sustain an authentic, faithful relationship to God. Kierkegaard thought that many people who called themselves Christians were living under an illusion, since they merely lived in a Christian society and followed its conventions. His writing aims to unsettle readers, to break through their complacent, comfortable veneer of religiosity, and to show that becoming a Christian is a demanding, arduous, and never-ending task. He takes care not to claim any kind of spiritual authority or superiority, counting himself along with all the others who fall short of the Christian ideal and face the task of becoming a Christian. For Kierkegaard, Christianity is not just difficult, but paradoxical, and he accentuates this in his writings. Instead of helping his readers to understand faith more clearly, he argues that genuine faith simply cannot be understood.

Kierkegaard was an enigmatic and complex character, and although he complained that he was misunderstood, as an author he is often deliberately elusive. His style of writing is engaging, and generally very readable, but his approach to subject-matter is rarely straightforward. Kierkegaard's best-known and most important philosophical books are written under a variety of pseudonyms. These pseudonymous texts are quite unlike other works of philosophy: they include different literary forms, such as stories and fictional diaries, and their philosophical content is frequently veiled in layers of irony. Another challenge to readers new to Kierkegaard is the fact that, despite his criticisms of philosophy, his texts are full of references to the philosophical tradition – particularly to ancient Greek philosophy, which he generally approved of, and to Hegel, his perennial adversary. And although Kierkegaard was not a theologian, and was not especially interested in elucidating Christian doctrine, his philosophy is intimately connected to theological concepts that may be unfamiliar to modern readers.

This book offers an accessible introduction to Kierkegaard's thought. But instead of simplifying his philosophy – which, in overlooking its subtlety and intricacy, would fail to do it justice – the chapters that follow will illuminate its difficult, perplexing aspects. They are unlikely to make Kierkegaard's philosophy effortlessly understandable: he writes about human life, and this is seldom easy to make sense of. But this book will at least help readers to appreciate Kierkegaard's contribution to philosophy, and encourage them to approach his texts with a better grasp of their background and significance, and with some idea of who their author was, and what he was trying to achieve.

We will focus mainly on the pseudonymous works that Kierkegaard published during the 1840s, rather than on the 'Edifying Discourses' and the later polemics against the Danish Church that were written in

his own name. This is not because these more explicitly Christian texts
are unimportant; on the contrary, they often echo the ideas expressed
in the pseudonymous works, and some readers find that Kierkegaard's
eloquent religious discourses provide a good way into his thought.
But the pseudonymous works tend to be more frequently read
and debated, and they have certainly had a greater impact on modern
philosophy.

Chapter 1 offers a short biography of Kierkegaard, an overview
of his authorship, and a discussion of the relationship between his
life and his works. Because Kierkegaard insists on writing from the
perspective of the 'existing individual', opposing the view that philosophy should or could be objective and detached, personal and intellectual elements in his work are much more closely intertwined than
in most philosophical texts. Kierkegaard's difficult relationship with
his father, his dissatisfaction with academic life, and his decision not
to marry his fiancée Regine Olsen, all provided material for his
philosophical reflections. His writing often has autobiographical
resonance, although it can be difficult to distinguish this from creative self-interpretation, or even self-fabrication.

The second chapter examines Kierkegaard's unique literary
style, exploring the way in which his methods of communication
are designed to have a particular effect on the reader. Because
Kierkegaard is not presenting a doctrine, a ready-made truth, but
trying to show the reader the truth about herself, his philosophy does
not take the form of a rational, systematic argument. He uses
pseudonyms, characters, situations and metaphors to dramatize his
ideas, showing how they are exemplified in human life; often the
reader is left to choose between the different possibilities presented
in the text. Furthermore, it is never clear whether the views expressed
by the pseudonyms can be attributed to Kierkegaard himself. In his
retrospective account of his authorship, *The Point of View for My
Work as An Author*, Kierkegaard describes his pseudonymous books
as attempts at 'indirect communication': this means that they seek to
remove the reader's illusions (such as the belief that she is already a
Christian) as well as lead her towards the truth.

This kind of communication is directed mainly at a certain
type of sophisticated, highly-educated reader, and amongst these
Kierkegaard was particularly concerned to provoke followers of
the great systematic philosopher, Hegel. Chapter 3 focuses on
Kierkegaard's critique of Hegel, which underlies his entire

philosophy. Although Kierkegaard's writing attacks Hegel, often rather polemically, it also exhibits his influence. This chapter offers a brief outline of some of Hegel's key ideas, before considering Kierkegaard's complex relationship to Hegelian philosophy. One question that needs to be addressed here is how well Kierkegaard understood Hegel: he probably read little of Hegel, relying instead on lectures given by his teachers at the University of Copenhagen. Moreover, Kierkegaard tended to conflate Hegelian philosophy with abstract thinking and academia in general, which he found pretentious, superficial and spiritually deadening. (This means that it is important to distinguish between the Hegel who is the target of Kierkegaard's texts, and the real Hegel who created a profound, original, and highly spiritual philosophy.) Kierkegaard's first book, *Either/Or*, exemplifies his idiosyncratic interpretation of Hegel, and a short discussion of this text shows how Kierkegaard's philosophy developed in response to Danish debates about Hegelian ideas.

Chapter 4 explores and clarifies one of the most important themes within Kierkegaard's thought: the notion of subjectivity. In his book *Concluding Unscientific Postscript* Kierkegaard suggests that 'subjectivity is truth'. This kind of truth is not an object of knowledge, but a way of existing authentically and faithfully. Kierkegaard asks how a person can be true – to herself, to another person, or to God – when life is continually changing and moving forwards. Connected to this account of subjective truth is Kierkegaard's distinction between different types of subjectivity, or different 'spheres of existence': the aesthetic, the ethical and the religious. As well as examining each of these approaches to life, and considering how a person can move from one kind of subjectivity to another, we will consider whether Kierkegaard's emphasis on subjectivity makes his view of human existence too individualistic.

Kierkegaard's interpretation of subjectivity involves the Christian notion of sin, and Chapter 5 focuses on this more theological aspect of his philosophy. As a Christian, Kierkegaard regards sin as a basic and ubiquitous feature of the human condition. This chapter begins by explaining the meaning of sin in general, and suggesting ways in which a non-Christian reader might be able to make sense of the idea that we are all sinners. Then we will turn to Kierkegaard's own analysis of sin in his books *The Concept of Anxiety* and *The Sickness Unto Death*. Instead of examining sin from a doctrinal, dogmatic point of view, these texts offer highly original and perceptive accounts of the psychological states connected to human sinfulness – and in particular they highlight an intimate relationship between sin and freedom. Kierkegaard's treatment of sin demonstrates how he manages to combine traditional religious ideas with a new and quite radical philosophical position.

Chapters 6 and 7 offer commentaries on two of Kierkegaard's best-known and most widely read books, *Fear and Trembling* and *Philosophical Fragments*. These commentaries bring together the issues and themes explored in previous chapters, and show how Kierkegaard's philosophical ideas and communicative methods are exemplified in specific texts. In *Fear and Trembling* Kierkegaard uses the biblical story of Abraham and Isaac to challenge Hegel's interpretation of religious faith, and to argue that Abraham's actions go against both reason and morality. He presents an uncompromising view of faith that emphasizes the individual's absolute duty to God, but he also suggests that faith gives people happiness in their ordinary, day-to-day lives. The commentary on *Philosophical Fragments* explores the notion of paradox that is at the heart of Kierkegaard's thought. In the *Fragments* he insists that the Christian doctrine of the incarnation – the teaching that in Jesus Christ God has lived a human life on earth – is absolutely paradoxical, and offensive to rational thought. For Kierkegaard, this means that previous philosophical concepts cannot do justice to the Christian's relationship to God.

The book ends by offering some reflections on Kierkegaard's thought as a whole, and by discussing its impact on subsequent philosophers. Kierkegaard's work, so firmly rooted in a religious view of life, inspired the God-less philosophies of thinkers like Sartre and the early Heidegger, and it is fascinating to see what happens to Kierkegaard's ideas when they become detached from their Christian context. It is also interesting to consider that European philosophy in the twentieth century, and perhaps also today, has been shaped above all by two nineteenth century writers who were ahead of their own time: Kierkegaard and Nietzsche. Whereas Kierkegaard insists that becoming a Christian is the highest path available to a person, Nietzsche attacks religion as both a symptom and a source of spiritual corruption. But both philosophers identify apathy and nihilism as the greatest dangers of modern life – and both produced astonishing and brilliant works of literature that offer a most unorthodox kind of guidance to those seeking meaning, freedom and happiness.

CHAPTER 1

KIERKEGAARD'S LIFE AND WORKS

KIERKEGAARD: A BRIEF BIOGRAPHY

Ane Kierkegaard gave birth to her seventh and last child in Copenhagen on 5 May, 1813, and the baby boy was named Søren Aabye. The child's father Michael – already middle-aged at the time of Søren's birth – was a successful businessman and a strict Lutheran Christian: life in the Kierkegaard household was both materially comfortable and spiritually austere. As a young boy Søren was sensitive and exceptionally bright, physically weak and slightly hunch-backed, and dressed in old-fashioned, tightly buttoned clothes. Not surprisingly he was sometimes bullied by other children – but instead of trying to win acceptance and popularity, he fought back with sarcastic, cruel and often very witty retorts. One of his schoolteachers described him as 'like a little old man', different from the other children and never quite fitting in. Many who knew Kierkegaard as a child, however, remembered him as cheerful, mischievous and very fond of jokes.

Søren's childhood seems to have been dominated by the rather forbidding presence of his melancholy, eccentric and increasingly reclusive father, who lavished attention – if not affection – on his youngest, cleverest son. This encouraged Søren's precocious intellectual development, but did little to strengthen his mental health. Instead of sending his child out to play, Michael Kierkegaard would conduct imaginary tours of Europe in his study, describing the history and architecture of a city in minute detail before leading Søren around the room and asking him to recount the views he saw – of Paris in one corner, of Florence in another. By the time Søren was seven years old, his father was teaching him logic by engaging him in conversation and then subjecting his responses to rigorous, critical analysis. When Michael Kierkegaard held dinner parties, which were attended by the intellectual and religious elite of Copenhagen, he allowed Søren to listen to the conversation that took place at the dinner table; afterwards he would tell the young boy to sit in each of the empty chairs and present the views and arguments of each guest in turn. Reflecting on his upbringing towards the end of his life, Søren Kierkegaard writes that his father's fault 'consisted not in a lack of love but in mistaking a child for an old man'[1].

As he grew older, Søren became increasingly aware of his father's gloomy, guilt-ridden religious attitude, and this made his own relationship to Christianity more complex and ambivalent. 'In a way I did love Christianity – to me it was the venerable – to be sure, it had made me extremely unhappy, humanly speaking. It was closely linked to my relationship with my father, the person I have most deeply loved. . .'[2] Søren believed that he, like many of his siblings, was destined to die prematurely; looking back on his childhood at the age of twenty-five, he wrote in his journal that

> I felt the stillness of death grow around me when I saw my father, an unhappy man who was to outlive us all, a cross on the tomb of all his hopes. There must be a guilt upon the whole family, the punishment of God must be on it . . . and only at times did I find a little relief in the thought that my father had been given the heavy task of comforting us with the consolation of religion, of ministering to us so that a better world should be open to us, even though we lost everything in this one.[3]

This idea that the family would be punished seems to be rooted in Michael Kierkegaard's confession of some guilty secrets to his son. One of these was that as a young boy he had, while looking after a flock of sheep out on the Jutland heath, fervently cursed God for his poor peasant life. Other, more sordid revelations – about which we can only speculate – probably included the fact that he had slept with his second wife Ane, who at the time was his servant, while his first wife was on her deathbed; and also that he had visited brothels where he had contracted syphilis. Søren described his discovery of the shady past of his pious, apparently virtuous father as a 'great earthquake'.

In 1830 Kierkegaard began to study theology at the University of Copenhagen, and planned to become a pastor (a Lutheran minister). This career path seemed natural, and was certainly in accordance with his father's wishes. Once at university, however, he neglected his theological studies in favour of philosophy, to which his thirst for ideas and his sharp, inquiring mind were perfectly suited. Kierkegaard was particularly drawn to Hegel's philosophy, which at that time was a new, radical and exciting system of thought, hotly debated by the Danish intelligentsia. Despite his enthusiasm for philosophy, Kierkegaard was often cynical towards his teachers and complained about their pretentiousness, superficiality and intellectual complacency. Like many people in their early twenties, Kierkegaard was concerned with questions about how best to live his life and which choices to make, and he felt frustrated when the academic study of philosophy – supposedly the pursuit of wisdom – failed to help him to address these fundamental questions.

Liberated to some extent from his father's oppressive influence, Kierkegaard experimented with a hedonistic, decadent lifestyle: he spent large sums of money on fashionable clothes, carriages and expensive cigars, and devoted most of his time to sitting in cafés or strolling through the streets of Copenhagen. He wore his hair swept high above his forehead (six inches, according to one acquaintance, although this is difficult to believe). He enjoyed entertaining people with his witty conversation, and he became a familiar and intriguing young man-about-town. One of his friends, Hans Brøchner, describes Kierkegaard during this time:

> There could be something infinitely gentle and loving in his eye, but also something stimulating and exasperating. With just a glance at a passer-by he could irresistibly 'establish a rapport' with him, as he expressed it. The person who received his look became either attracted or repelled, embarrassed, uncertain, or exasperated. I have walked the whole length of a street with him while he explained how it was possible to carry out psychological studies by establishing such a rapport with the passer-by. And while he expanded on the theory he realised it in practice with nearly everyone we met. There was no one on whom his glance did not make a visible impression . . . It was always interesting to accompany him, but there was a difficulty of sorts in walking with him. Because of the irregularity of his movements, which must

have been related to his lopsidedness, it was never possible to keep in a straight line while walking with him; one was always being pushed, successively, either in towards the houses and the cellar stairwells, or out towards the gutters. When, in addition, he also gestured with his arms and his rattan cane, it became even more of an obstacle course. Once in a while, it was necessary to take the opportunity to switch around to his other side in order to gain sufficient space.[4]

Kierkegaard did very little work – in a letter to his brother-in-law, he wrote, 'I am embarked on studies for the theological examination, a pursuit which does not interest me in the least and which therefore is not going especially well'. From a psychological point of view these student years were unstable, oscillating frequently between exuberance and despair. He went through phases of depression that made everything seem pointless: 'I don't care for anything. I don't care to ride, that involves too much movement; I don't care to walk, that is too fatiguing; I don't care to lie down, for either I must remain there, and that I don't care for, or else I must get up again, and that I don't care for at all. The sum of it all is, I don't care'. At these times he felt paralysed, incapable of really *doing* anything, perhaps because his life was too narrowly intellectual. For several years Kierkegaard drifted in academia, delaying his theological exams and contemplating his future with uncertainty.

1838 was an important year for Kierkegaard. On 19 May – shortly after his twenty-fifth birthday – he had a profound spiritual experience, 'an indescribable joy' that changed his sense of himself and of his place in the world. This experience gave him a renewed religious inspiration: he wrote in his journal that 'I will strive to come into a far more inward relationship to Christianity; for until now I have in a way been always standing outside it, have contended for its truth; in a purely outward way I have borne Christ's cross'. Three months later Michael Kierkegaard died, at the age of eighty-one, leaving a huge fortune to his two remaining sons. Although he no longer needed to earn a living, Kierkegaard's response to his father's death was finally to apply himself seriously to his theological studies.

During the next two years Kierkegaard worked hard, passing his exams and beginning to train as a pastor. He also met and fell in love with a teenage girl, ten years younger than himself, called Regine

Olsen. Regine liked Kierkegaard too, and they embarked on a formal courtship that, although physically chaste, was no doubt emotionally intense. Their relationship had a strong intellectual element, with Kierkegaard assuming the role of teacher – he sent Regine books and often read to her, and he liked to discuss philosophical and spiritual ideas at length, making sure she understood everything correctly. As the months went by Regine became more aware of Kierkegaard's sensitivity and tendency to melancholy, but this seems only to have increased her love for him. When Kierkegaard asked her to marry him in 1840, she accepted immediately.

Very soon, however, Kierkegaard changed his mind. Although he loved Regine, he felt that married life was not for him – perhaps because he thought it was incompatible with his spiritual aspirations, perhaps because he feared emotional and sexual intimacy, perhaps because he felt that he was too depressive to be a good husband. Kierkegaard believed that marriage required complete openness between husband and wife, and he feared that sharing his darker side would place too heavy a burden on Regine. Although he loved her – even, it seemed to him, *because* he loved her, and did not want her to suffer – he decided that he had to end the engagement, and tried to do so gently, but Regine (and her family) found this difficult to understand and accept. Breaking up was a drawn-out and painful process for both of them, and when the relationship was finally and definitely over Kierkegaard left Copenhagen for Berlin, presumably to escape from a messy situation for which he was wholly responsible. He also abandoned his plan to become a pastor.

This episode changed the direction of Kierkegaard's life, both inwardly and outwardly. His relationship with Regine had led him to a crisis of decision, where he realized that he had to take full responsibility for a choice that would really affect another person, as well as himself. He also found himself confronted with a moral dilemma, for in order to resolve his inner conflict he had either to break his promise to a girl who loved him, or follow a course of action that now felt wrong. The choice he made exposed him to the judgements of others, who thought that he had treated Regine terribly. In breaking off the engagement Kierkegaard was not simply rejecting Regine – he regarded her as his ideal, and was certainly not interested in getting involved with anyone else – but cutting himself off from the possibility of a respectable, conventional life as a husband, father and pastor. Instead, he would devote himself to writing. Although this writing turned out to have a dramatic impact on others – even within his own lifetime, and much more so in the twentieth century – Kierkegaard regarded his literary work as a withdrawal from life. He chose for his first pseudonym the Latin name 'Victor Eremita', which means something like 'Triumphant Recluse' or 'Solitary Champion'.

Kierkegaard stayed in Berlin for several months, attending lectures on philosophy – particularly Hegelian philosophy – and writing a lengthy manuscript, into which he incorporated a lot of material from his earlier journals. This was to become his first major published work, *Either/Or*. He felt increasingly disillusioned with philosophy, for his experience with Regine had made him more intensely aware of the inadequacy of a purely rational approach to life. How, he wondered, can logic and reasoning help a person to make a choice between two alternatives which are both, in different ways, wrong? How can intellectual knowledge provide a basis for decisions concerning the future, which is always *unknown*? Reflecting on his failure to commit to marriage and to an ordinary career, Kierkegaard found that his situation presented a philosophical problem that philosophy itself seemed unable to cope with: how should we use our freedom?

Either/Or, which Kierkegaard published in February 1843, addresses this question of freedom by setting up an opposition between three different kinds of life – the aesthetic, the ethical and the religious. The text combines philosophical insight, and in particular a critique of Hegelian ideas, with fictional and autobiographical material. It is a complicated, confusing and sometimes tedious book, divided into two substantial, densely written volumes. (When I read it for the first time, shortly after deciding to write a PhD on Kierkegaard, my heart sank as I wondered what I had let myself in for.) The first volume, described as 'aesthetic', is supposedly written by an unknown young man; this includes various essays, aphorisms, fragments of prose and an extract from a personal journal called 'Diary of a Seducer'. The aesthete has an experimental approach to life: he seeks pleasure and novelty, lacks a clear purpose, and often complains that he is unhappy (he is rather like Kierkegaard had been as a student). The second volume, described as 'ethical', contains two extremely long and rather boring letters that appear to have been written by an older man called Judge

William, who disapproves of the aesthetic attitude and encourages the young man to take responsibility for his life. This volume also includes a sermon about love, freedom and the individual's relationship to God. We are told that this sermon, which comes right at the end of the book, is written by an elderly country pastor: it represents the religious point of view. In the preface to the book, the pseudonymous author Victor Eremita describes how he found its contents hidden in the secret drawer of an old writing desk. The reader of *Either/Or* is left to puzzle over and reflect on the contrasting points of view expressed by the different voices within the book – for Kierkegaard wants us to think for ourselves, not only about the central philosophical question of freedom, but about how this relates to our own lives.

1843 was an astonishingly creative and productive year for Kierkegaard: his ideas had been building up for a long time, and now they were 'cascading down upon me: healthy, happy, thriving, blessed children, born of ease and yet all of them with the birthmark of my personality'. By the end of the year he had published, in addition to *Either/Or*, two more pseudonymous books, *Fear and Trembling* and *Repetition*, and also three collections of 'Edifying Discourses', written under his own name. Although *Fear and Trembling* and *Repetition* were written under different pseudonyms, they were published on the same day, and make most sense when read as companion pieces: they both present an ethical dilemma; they both explore the issues of faith or fidelity, loss, and suffering; and they both suggest that rational thought is incapable of grasping the whole of human existence. *Repetition* describes a broken engagement, while *Fear and Trembling* explores the biblical story of Abraham and Isaac.

For the rest of his life Kierkegaard spent most of his time writing. He worked at home, standing at his tall writing desk or pacing about the room as he thought through his ideas. The style of his writing is as important as its content, since it aims to unsettle, to provoke and to persuade the reader, and Kierkegaard would read aloud to himself as he wrote, trying out the rhythm and rhetorical impact of his sentences. Although he was so often alone, he had a very sociable side to his character and liked to take a break from his work by going for long walks through the city. He became well-known in Copenhagen for his literary work as well as for his eccentric personality (it did not take people long to figure out who was behind the pseudonymous books), and he had many acquaintances with whom he would stop to talk when he happened to meet them on the street. Kierkegaard's reputation was severely damaged, however, when in 1845 he provoked a satirical magazine called *The Corsair* into attacking him: he published a letter criticizing the magazine and its editors, and for months afterwards *The Corsair* printed humiliating caricatures of Kierkegaard in his large top-hat and badly fitting trousers. Now, when he went out walking, shopkeepers and passers-by laughed at him and children taunted him. What is strange – and interesting – about the '*Corsair* Affair' is that Kierkegaard deliberately sought this abuse and ridicule.

During the 1840s Kierkegaard was particularly prolific, and his most important philosophical works were written between 1843 and 1849. These include (in addition to the three books of 1843) *Philosophical Fragments*, which discusses the Christian doctrine of the incarnation; *The Concept of Anxiety*, an elaborate analysis of the idea of original sin; *Concluding Unscientific Postscript to the Philosophical Fragments*, an enormous book about 'the problem of becoming a Christian'; and *The Sickness Unto Death*, which explores the psychological experience of despair and suggests that this can only be overcome through a Christian life of faith and forgiveness. All of these books were published under various pseudonyms, and as their titles suggest they do not tend to make for light reading. *Concluding Unscientific Postscript* which, like *Philosophical Fragments* is written under the pseudonym Johannes Climacus, includes a review of the previous pseudonymous texts and discusses their aims and methods collectively. This book ends with a section signed by Kierkegaard himself, headed 'A First and Last Explanation', in which he acknowledges that he is the author of all the pseudonymous works, and explains his own relationship to the pseudonyms.

Kierkegaard also continued to publish regular collections of 'Edifying Discourses' under his own name, and these religious essays which, like sermons, take a short biblical text as their point of departure, are more accessible than the pseudonymous works, although they tend to be less widely read by those interested in Kierkegaard's philosophy. Their content is not, however, unrelated to the pseudonymous literature. From 1850 until the end of his life, Kierkegaard's writing became increasingly polemical and he published several attacks on contemporary Christianity and on prominent, highly respected members of the Danish Church. These polemics which, like the religious discourses, are written in Kierkegaard's own name, caused a great deal of controversy (no doubt to their author's satisfaction) and generated much debate throughout Scandinavia. In 1854 Kierkegaard set up a magazine called *The Moment* (to which he was the only contributor), and every issue was more or less devoted to complaining that his fellow 'Christians' were inauthentic, hypocritical and corrupt. The tone of these later works is bitter and highly-strung, and they do not have the philosophical interest and importance of the earlier publications.

Kierkegaard died in 1855, at the age of forty-two. In contrast to the mood of his last writings, this relatively early death was dignified and serene. After collapsing in the street in the autumn of 1855, he admitted himself to hospital and died there a few weeks later, on 11 November. Those who visited him in the days leading up to his death were struck by his composure and particularly by his radiant eyes. Kierkegaard's simple will stated that his few possessions should go to Regine Olsen. The funeral was attended by a large crowd of people, including a group of protestors – readers of *The Moment* – who claimed that the Church was hypocritical to bury a dissenter such as Kierkegaard on consecrated ground.

When Kierkegaard's brother Peter went to empty his apartment soon after his death, he found a large, neatly arranged pile of papers, including twenty-six notebooks, thirty-six volumes of personal journals, and the latest, yet-to-be published issue of *The Moment*. There was also a manuscript entitled *The Point of View for My Work as an Author*, in which Kierkegaard offers a retrospective explanation of his authorship and claims that his diverse publications share a common purpose: to make people aware of what Christianity really means. This book was published posthumously in 1859, and over the next few years scholars took on the task of deciphering, organizing and editing the notes and journals, which often shed light on the books that were published during Kierkegaard's lifetime.

PARALLELS BETWEEN KIERKEGAARD'S LIFE AND PHILOSOPHY

In the case of most philosophers it is quite easy to separate their intellectual work from their personal lives. This is because philosophers tend to address universal questions – such as whether God exists; what can (and what cannot) be known, and how we are able to know it; how to make ethical judgements, and so on – and they aim to provide answers that will be relevant and useful to everybody. For this reason philosophers are expected to put to one side their personal interests, opinions and prejudices, and to concentrate on what all human beings have in common, regardless of when and where they happen to live. This may be difficult or even impossible to achieve in practice, but nevertheless it provides philosophers with a model or an ideal of intellectual clarity. 'Philosophy' means the love of wisdom, and clarity of thought is an invaluable tool for attaining wisdom and, even more importantly, for communicating it to others. Most philosophical texts present a view of the world or of human nature in the form of a rational argument. Traditionally in philosophy, rational thought is regarded as the most important aspect of human nature, because through the use of reason people are able to reach reliable, stable conclusions. Because we all share a capacity for rational thought, reason provides guidelines for debate and a basis for consensus. Conventional philosophical method attempts to exclude what is personal, or subjective, and to pursue truths that are unaffected by particular experiences or conditions. The life story of a philosopher may be interesting, but it is not usually essential for understanding his or her thought.

Kierkegaard, however, is not like most philosophers. One of the aims of his authorship is to challenge the traditional ideal of philosophy as impersonal and objective, and he pours his own life – his personality, his emotions, his deepest concerns – into his writing. Instead of excluding his personal life from his intellectual work, he turned his experiences of love, suffering, spiritual weakness, moral conflict and despair into philosophical problems, and insisted that these could not be addressed through rational, abstract thought. Kierkegaard argues that objectivity is dishonest and unable to capture what is most fundamental to human existence, because before anybody becomes a philosopher – and even, in fact, before they start to think about anything – they are already an 'existing individual' who lives, breathes and moves continually closer to death. The idea of the 'existing individual' is absolutely central to Kierkegaard's philosophy, but of course this is more than just an idea, and abstract concepts fail to capture the vitality and fluidity of life. The truth of every existing individual is only known from the inside, as it is actually lived. This means that subjective human existence has to be understood not only as an idea within Kierkegaard's philosophy, but also as the perspective from which that philosophy was written.

For readers and students of Kierkegaard, then, the details of his life and the relationship between his life and his work are particularly significant. He himself suggested that 'the day will come when not only my writings, but precisely my life – the intriguing secret of all the machinery – will be studied and studied'. It is not always easy to make a clear distinction between Kierkegaard's experience of personal (or 'existential') problems and his presentation of philosophical problems. His most basic question is about how to live a happy, meaningful life, which is for him inseparable from the question of how to become a true Christian. In a sense there is nothing new about this 'existential' orientation: it is the root of philosophical inquiry from which all other questions take their significance and urgency. Socrates, one of the earliest and most influential thinkers in the Western tradition, certainly practised philosophy in this way. However, Kierkegaard felt that philosophy in nineteenth-century Europe had become a dry, shallow, lifeless pursuit which, with its abstract concepts and theories, had failed to take account of the particular thinker. It is possible to think about philosophical questions without really bringing *oneself* into question; it is possible to seek knowledge and truth whilst ignoring Socrates' advice to 'know yourself'. Kierkegaard argues that any philosophy which does not include reflection on oneself is a deception, a distraction from the pursuit of genuine wisdom. This raises questions about how we, as Kierkegaard's readers, respond to his books, for his philosophy has an unusually intimate relationship to each of our existences as well as to his own life – but we will set aside these questions until the following chapter.

There are several areas in which the parallels between Kierkegaard's life and his thought are particularly striking, and we shall now explore these one by one. It is important to bear in mind, however, that recognizing such parallels is not the same as claiming that Kierkegaard's thought is completely, or even primarily, shaped by personal concerns. There are also philosophical and theological reasons for the positions that are outlined below. For the time being, though, we are focusing on a biographical perspective.

(i) Conflict between intellectual and spiritual life

Kierkegaard was aware of an inner tension between his extremely reflective, analytical mind and his passionate religious sensibilities. In other words, he experienced a conflict between his head and his heart. Recalling his childhood in *The Point of View for My Work as an Author*, he states that 'I began at once with reflection . . . I am reflection, from first to last'. He was ambivalent about his exceptional intellectual powers, because although he used them to protect himself from his detractors, to gain respect and social status, and ultimately to achieve success as a writer, he often felt trapped within abstract thought. He could play with all sorts of ideas and hypotheses in his mind, but he felt incapable of bringing any of them into being, of turning possibilities into something actual and concrete. Kierkegaard knew that taking refuge in intellectual reflection was a way of dealing with the difficulties of life, and particularly with human interaction: 'in desperate despair I grasped at nothing but the intellectual side in man and clung fast to it, so that the thought of my own considerable powers of mind was my only consolation, ideas my one joy, and mankind indifferent to me'.

Kierkegaard's sense of being too narrowly confined by his intellect was especially acute during his ten years at the University of Copenhagen. He often felt disgusted by academia, which he describes in one journal entry as 'this dreadful still life, so miserable and thin a life'. Several years later he was able to take a more balanced view of abstract thought, condemning not reflection itself but 'a standstill in reflection' as 'the fraud and the corruption' of existence. There remains, however, a strong connection between Kierkegaard's personal experience of academic life and his philosophical claim that mere concepts cannot encompass and express the whole of existence. Throughout his authorship, and particularly in the pseudonymous works, Kierkegaard argues that the intellect has to surrender in order for passion and faith – essential elements of the religious life – to be possible. His own failure to find fulfilment in academic work helps to explain why, despite his considerable intellectual interests and abilities, he expresses such anti-intellectualism.

(ii) The individual's relationship to others

Kierkegaard's philosophy, and especially his account of religious faith, are notoriously individualistic. Kierkegaard challenges the view, which in his time had been made popular by Hegel's philosophy, that the individual finds purpose and fulfilment by participating in a community. This emphasis on being a part of a larger whole can be applied to secular or religious life: the state and the church both provide an institution within which every member can contribute something. In the case of the church, each individual's relationship to God is mediated by sacred texts, by customary rituals, by members of the clergy, and by contact with fellow believers.

Kierkegaard argues, however, that faith is a purely inward and private affair, and that everybody stands alone before God. He also suggests that it is impossible for one individual genuinely to understand and to communicate with another. Out in the world, we present a certain public self and we judge others according to how they appear, but in relation to God we become transparent – and it is only in this relationship that we are seen as we really are, and can truly express ourselves. Kierkegaard is not the first Christian writer to make this sharp distinction between the external, social world and the inner, spiritual world, but in his case this view also reflects his personal experience of being an outsider, of never quite fitting in with the crowd, and of feeling misunderstood by others. His tendency to set himself apart from conventional life became decisive when he rejected marriage and a career in the church. This is not to suggest that Kierkegaard disapproved of ordinary life and of personal relationships – on the contrary, he admired people who were able to live contentedly with others. He certainly did not deny that love of one's neighbour is an indispensable aspect of Christian life. The point is rather that he found close human relationships difficult, and that he turned this difficulty into a philosophical problem about the possibility of authentic communication.

(iii) The question of freedom

Freedom is a perennial philosophical question. There is an ongoing debate between philosophers about how to define freedom and about how much freedom human beings have. For Kierkegaard, to be free means to be capable of making a decision and to act upon it. This may seem straightforward enough, but Kierkegaard often points out that it is possible to live without ever really acknowledging and expressing one's power of choice. Although someone might follow their desires, choosing to watch a particular film or to eat a particular piece of cake, they are not yet free if they have not chosen *themselves* – chosen what kind of person to be, what kind of life to live. In *Either/Or* the pseudonym Judge William argues that in order to be free we must continually choose, or repeatedly commit to, a purpose or a direction in life. Judge William illustrates this idea with the metaphor of a captain steering a ship: if the captain takes a break and lets the ship drift for a while, then he has given up his freedom, relinquished his responsibility, because he is allowing the past to determine his future. Because we live in time – represented in Judge William's analogy by the current of the sea and the force of the wind – we are always in motion, but if one wants to *move oneself* one has to choose a direction and steer attentively towards it.

This idea of self-choice is difficult to make sense of (and even more difficult to live up to). But what is interesting about Kierkegaard's view of freedom is that it involves the idea of inward power – exercising freedom is not simply a matter of being unconstrained by external forces, but of having a kind of spiritual momentum within oneself. This interpretation of freedom invokes a distinction between strength and weakness. This, in turn, is linked to the question of happiness: when we are depressed we feel weak, unable to cope with life, whereas when we are happy we feel capable of anything. Kierkegaard's understanding of freedom in terms of power and happiness comes from his own experience of weakness and melancholy, which he sometimes described as a feeling of paralysis. His relationship with Regine is important in this respect, for having made a decision to marry her he found himself incapable of following it through. He regarded this failure as a kind of spiritual impotence. On the other hand, Kierkegaard *did* make a choice not to marry – and this was not an easy decision once he was engaged – and through this choice he took responsibility for the direction of his life. In his book *Repetition*, which tells the story of a young man who changes his mind about marrying his fiancée, Kierkegaard presents the decision to break off the engagement as a moment of self-discovery and a realization of freedom.

(iv) Suffering

As we have seen, Kierkegaard experienced much suffering in his life. His sensitive temperament and his tendencies to melancholy and anxiety, his difficult relationships with his father and with Regine, and the fact that by the age of twenty-five he had lost his parents and five of his siblings, gave Kierkegaard an intimate understanding of various kinds of psychological pain. Rather than avoiding or denying it, Kierkegaard was unusually willing to confront and to investigate his suffering. (Perhaps he even invited it at times by deliberately setting himself at odds with people – for example, by provoking the editors of *The Corsair* to attack him.) Kierkegaard's sensitivity to suffering extended to others as well as to himself: one of his friends remembered that 'he gave consolation not by covering up sorrow, but by first making one genuinely aware of it, by bringing it to complete clarity'.

The theme of suffering is present throughout Kierkegaard's authorship. To some extent this can be explained by Kierkegaard's religious perspective – after all, one of the most important images of Christian faith is the cross, which symbolizes a heavy burden and a slow, painful death. From a spiritual point of view, suffering is an inevitable part of life and must be accepted and endured when it presents itself, not turned away from. Because Kierkegaard is concerned with 'the task of becoming a Christian', he has to address the question of how to respond to the painful and difficult aspects of life. However, his persistent emphasis on suffering, and the way he makes this absolutely central to his interpretation of religious faith, is striking even compared to other Christian writers. He is especially fascinated by biblical characters such as Abraham and Job, who suffer because of the loss – or, at least, the threat of loss – of what is most precious to them. In fact, many of the myths and stories that Kierkegaard uses to present his philosophical ideas feature characters who lose and grieve for someone they love.

Many philosophers regard suffering as an obstacle to religious belief, and even as an argument against the existence of God. They ask, 'how can we believe that a loving, all-powerful God created a world like this one, so full of suffering'? (And of course, it is not just philosophers who raise this question.) This presents theologians with the task of reconciling belief in a perfect, omnipotent God with the fact that life is so often unsatisfactory. For Kierkegaard, suffering poses a slightly different problem, because he is not so much concerned with the objective fact of God's existence or non-existence, but with the indvidual's subjective relationship to God. He suggests that in order to love God one has to accept suffering, to sacrifice one's expectation of happiness for the sake of a higher spiritual life. It is possible, though not easy, to love God in this way. It is much harder, however, to endure suffering and to continue to believe that one is *loved by God*, that God cares about the specific details of one's own life, and to regard this painful, difficult life as a gift from God. Even in the midst of suffering, the person who believes in this way feels blessed. This kind of faith, says Kierkegaard, does not make sense, and cannot be based on reason – but it is the very highest form of spirituality.

(v) Remaining faithful in spite of change

For Kierkegaard, faith is not just a matter of believing in something, but of *being true* to something – to God, to another person, to oneself, or to a particular vocation or ideal. In breaking off his engagement to Regine, Kierkegaard felt that he was guilty of betrayal and infidelity. He had failed to be true to a very important and meaningful promise, and for years afterwards he sought to come to terms with this intellectually. In a sense the situation had been beyond his control, because his engagement to Regine had been sincere and only after making the commitment did he feel that marriage would be a mistake. This experience made Kierkegaard acutely aware of being – like every other existing individual – in a process of becoming, of changing. How, then, is it possible to make promises and commitments when we know that we may later change our minds? What provides the basis for the constancy and stability of a faithful relationship to someone, or to something, when existence itself is always in motion? How can such an existence be *true*?

One of Kierkegaard's most important and original contributions to philosophy is an account of truth that is based on becoming, change and subjectivity. The kind of truth that belongs to existence is not something that is fixed, eternally-valid and objective, but a quality of life that is continually brought into being as that life is lived. In order to be true to something, one must not resist change and the flow of time, but must repeatedly renew one's commitment. In *Fear and Trembling* Kierkegaard emphasizes that Abraham's faith in God is renewed in every step he takes on his long journey to Mount Moriah, where, according to God's instructions, he is to sacrifice his son. Abraham's journey provides a metaphor for life: fidelity, constancy and truthfulness are the product of a dynamic process.

(vi) The search for meaning

Until Kierkegaard committed himself to his literary vocation, he often expressed a desire to find a purpose and a direction that would give shape and meaning to his life. He was searching for 'an idea for which I can live and die'. It was his own experience of despair and emptiness, and his dissatisfaction with a hedonistic lifestyle, that made him realize the dangers of nihilism (the refusal or the inability to find meaning and value in life, manifested in attitudes of indifference, cynicism or boredom). Kierkegaard encountered nihilism not only in himself, during his periods of melancholy, but in the culture of nineteenth-century Europe. He attacks the apathy of his contemporaries in his book *Two Ages*, where he writes that 'the age in which we live is wretched, because it is without passion'.

In the twentieth century nihilism came to be recognized as a pervasive cultural malaise, and as an urgent philosophical problem. Whereas philosophers had once devoted their attention to subjects such as logic, metaphysics, epistemology and ethics, many now took on the task of finding meaning and value in life – or, for those who felt that nihilism was inevitable, of working out how best to cope with it. This philosophical project – which is still ongoing – was largely inspired by Kierkegaard and Nietzsche, who both, independently of one another, brought the problem of nihilism to light. The character of the aesthete in *Either/Or* exemplifies the nihilistic attitude: he is unable to commit to any particular thing because nothing seems more worthwhile than anything else, and his life appears empty and meaningless. Judge William's letters to the aesthete are the first of many modern attempts to propose a solution to nihilism.

3. WHO IS THE 'REAL' KIERKEGAARD?

There is no doubt that Kierkegaard's personal experiences affected his philosophical concerns. But although it is important to be aware of the connection between his life and his work, it is also important to tread carefully – because we have to ask how much we really *know* about Kierkegaard's life. In a sense, all biographies are problematic because human beings are neither simple nor transparent, and the events of their lives, the testimonies of their acquaintances, and even their own views of themselves will not give complete access to their inner lives. The evidence will always be partial. Kierkegaard's biography is particularly questionable, for a number of reasons.

First, central to Kierkegaard's philosophy is the idea that the most real, most authentic part of a person is inward and invisible to others. This is partly a religious, and especially a Protestant, idea: our inner being is hidden from everyone except God, and only God is able to make a judgement about our true worth. It is also a version of the traditional philosophical distinction between appearance and reality: many philosophers, such as Plato and Kant, have argued that the world is not in fact the way it seems to be. Questioning appearances and refusing to take things at face value is an important aspect of philosophical method. For Kierkegaard the contrast between external appearances and inward truth is most significant in the case of human beings and, as we have seen, he believes that it is impossible for one person really to understand another. 'True inwardness demands absolutely no outward sign', writes the pseudonym Johannes Climacus in *Concluding Unscientific Postscript*. How, then, are we to know the truth about Kierkegaard's inwardness – which, according to his own philosophical view, is his authentic life – when all we have are the outward signs of his writing, the writings of others, and a few bare facts?

Second, even if we put this question to one side, or find a satisfactory response to it, we cannot assume that the pseudonymous authors of Kierkegaard's books represent his own views. Even though these texts contain material that appears to be autobiographical and confessional, the fact that Kierkegaard did not write them in his own name means that we cannot rely on them as revelations of his own inner life. However, it is by no means clear that the works published under Kierkegaard's name are any more genuinely representative of his position. They may well be less so: people usually avoid publicizing those aspects of themselves that they consider to be unattractive, weak, shallow, immoral, trivial, conceited, and so on.

We may feel tempted to look to Kierkegaard's private, unpublished journals for evidence of his authentic self. Again, though, this is problematic. Kierkegaard used his journals to record his philosophical ideas as well as his personal thoughts, and there is no way to distinguish between these with any certainty. For example, there are many similarities between comments in Kierkegaard's journals and the writings of the aesthete in *Either/Or* – does this mean that the aesthete resembles Kierkegaard, or that the journal entries are rough notes for *Either/Or*? Another problem with personal diaries, even if they do accurately record the writer's thoughts and experiences, is that they are very selective. The diarist includes what he or she thinks is most important, and may leave out information that a biographer would consider invaluable. As anyone who keeps a diary knows, a journal is a patchy and often disproportionately gloomy representation of life: when one feels happy, or is simply too busy, pages are left blank, whereas suffering and conflict may be described at great length.

Third, we have to consider the way in which Kierkegaard created himself through his writing. The relationship between his life and his works is not one-way: it is not only a matter of the life producing the work, but of the work producing the life. The 'historical' Kierkegaard whom we encounter through his authorship may in fact be a romanticized myth. For example, Kierkegaard presents his own interpretations of the broken engagement in texts like *Repetition*, and also in his private journals, but perhaps his decision not to marry was less spiritual, less tragic, and less interesting than these interpretations suggest – perhaps he simply went off Regine, or was unwilling to make the compromises that marriage requires. Constructing a glamorous, intriguing self-image can be for one's own benefit as well as for others – maybe we all do this to some extent, and in this way give meaning to our lives. Kierkegaard spent such a large proportion of his adult life writing that it must have been difficult even for him to tell the difference between 'himself' and his work. Did Kierkegaard control his writing, or did his writing control – or at least mould – him? Whereas twentieth-century biographers of Kierkegaard accepted his own version of his life, more recent biographers have been critical of the romantic myth and have drawn attention to the process of self-invention that occurs through the authorship.

It is up to Kierkegaard's readers how far to pursue the connections between his philosophy and his life. It is quite possible to read and discuss his books without knowledge of or reference to their author, and even if we acknowledge the influence of certain psychological factors Kierkegaard's philosophy should never simply be reduced to these. Even from a purely philosophical point of view, however, Kierkegaard's refusal to detach his own existence from his intellectual work is significant, since it questions and reaches beyond the limits that philosophy has traditionally imposed upon itself.

CHAPTER 2

THE QUESTION OF COMMUNICATION

INDIRECT COMMUNICATION

All books communicate something. The authors of philosophical books attempt to communicate truth, or wisdom: this might focus very narrowly on a specific topic, or it may encompass the whole universe. Whenever we read a philosophical text, we need to ask ourselves what kind of truth the writer is communicating, before figuring out our own responses to it. In the case of Kierkegaard's authorship, we are told – although this is not always obvious – that the matter in question is the truth of Christianity. For Kierkegaard, Christianity is not essentially a set of beliefs such as the existence of God, human immortality, or the divinity of Jesus Christ, or even a set of practices such as praying or taking communion, but a way of living one's life inwardly in relationship to God. This means that the truth of Christianity is a truth belonging to each individual's existence. Kierkegaard's books attempt to communicate to the reader the truth about her own life.

This kind of truth is not ready-made: it is not a doctrine, a list of facts, or a set of instructions. Because a person's life is a dynamic process, the truth of this life also takes the form of a movement, and is open-ended. It does not come from the outside, but from within each individual. The task of communicating this wisdom, then, is not a matter of placing before readers an objective, ready-made truth, but of awakening within them a willingness and an ability to see themselves clearly. Only when one understands one's own situation can one respond freely to it, doing what needs to be done and changing what needs to be changed. Kierkegaard's priority as a writer is to make his reader aware that he or she *exists*. He believed that most of his contemporaries lived under the illusion that they were already Christians simply by virtue of the fact that they belonged to a Christian society, and he wanted to remove this illusion so that people understood that they, as individuals, faced the task of *becoming* Christians.

When we open one of Kierkegaard's books for the first time we are likely to feel perplexed. This might be because we are new to philosophy, and are not yet familiar with the classical problems and the technical vocabulary. Even if we are experts in philosophy, however, the text will be strange and confusing. Of course, all philosophers have their own style of writing, which is more or less difficult to understand, but this style is usually secondary to the content of the text – to the ideas and arguments it presents. We generally expect a philosophical text to put forward a single, coherent point of view that we can assume is the author's own. But because Kierkegaard is concerned with communicating a subjective, existential kind of truth, he uses all sorts of different literary techniques that are intended to have an effect on the reader. These include fictional characters and situations, interpretations of biblical texts, metaphors and of course pseudonymous authors. As well as ordinary prose, some texts include letters, diaries and aphorisms. A single text often contains several different authors with conflicting points of view, without explaining which should be accepted and which rejected. In *Either/Or*, for example, the reader is presented with a choice between two different attitudes to life, and one of the effects of this is that the reader realizes that she does in fact *have* a choice. In other words, the style of the book as well as its content helps to make the reader aware of her own freedom.

Kierkegaard writes a lot about his own writing, and he is very self-conscious about his relationship to his reader. (He always refers to his 'reader', rather than his 'readers', to emphasize his desire to address 'the single, existing individual'.) At several points he discusses the question of communication, particularly in *Concluding Unscientific Postscript*, written under the pseudonym Johannes Climacus, and in the posthumously published *The Point of View for My Work as An Author*. Both of these books highlight a distinction between 'direct' and 'indirect' communication, and suggest that Kierkegaard's pseudonymous works are examples of indirect communication.

According to Kierkegaard (or to Johannes Climacus), indirect communication is necessary when the truth to be communicated is subjective – a quality within the reader – as opposed to objective.

The distinction between direct and indirect communication is connected to the distinction between objective and subjective knowledge. Objective knowledge basically means information, and information can be passed directly from one person to another. Subjective knowledge or self-knowledge, on the other hand, is not gained simply by gathering information about oneself, for it involves a turning-inward, a shift in perspective. Kierkegaard suggests that when the aim of communication is self-knowledge, the reader must go through a process of 'double reflection': she first understands the text at an intellectual level, and then relates this understanding to her own existence. In this way the text illuminates the reader's inner being.

Kierkegaard regards Socrates as an expert in indirect communication. Socrates taught wisdom – as Johannes Climacus puts it, he was 'a teacher of the ethical' – but he did not communicate with his students by presenting them with a theory or a doctrine. Instead, he would engage them in conversation, and ask them a series of questions that would eventually lead them to speak the truth themselves. Socrates' role can be compared to that of a midwife: the midwife does not give birth herself or present the mother with a baby, but helps her to give birth to what is already inside her. Similarly, Socrates did not present his listeners with a ready-made truth, but helped them to realize and to articulate wisdom that in fact they already possessed. There is of course an important difference between the midwife's work and Socrates' method: the mother who is giving birth knows that her child is inside her, and knows more or less what to expect by the end of her labour, whilst Socrates' student is usually ignorant of the fact that he can find the truth within himself, and is often taken by surprise during the process of learning.

Socrates wanted to encourage his students to discover the truth for themselves – for only then would their knowledge be genuine wisdom – and he did not want them to become disciples who simply believed whatever he said. Philosophy calls for independent, critical thought: if we accept something as true purely on the basis of someone else's authority, then we are not practising philosophy. Socrates refused to present himself as a learned man who was in possession of the truth; on the contrary, he repeatedly insisted that he was ignorant. He wanted to discourage people from relying on his authority and revering him – from looking at him instead of looking within themselves. For this reason, suggests Johannes Climacus,

Socrates considered his unattractive appearance (he was notoriously ugly) to be an advantage in his role as a teacher:

> He perceived that it might help to place the learner at a distance so that he would not be caught in a direct relation to his teacher, perhaps would admire him, perhaps would have his clothes made in the same way, but might understand through the repulsion of opposition . . . that the learner essentially has himself to deal with, and that the inwardness of truth is not the chummy inwardness with which two bosom friends walk arm in arm, but is the separation in which each person for himself is existing in what is true.[1]

In order to understand Kierkegaard's own strategies of indirect communication, we need to consider who he wanted to communicate with. The pseudonymous books, which include discussions of art, literature and philosophy, are aimed at a sophisticated, educated, cultured readership. Many of these readers would be academics, or at least people who regarded themselves as intellectuals. Kierkegaard thought that it was this group of people who were most completely deluded about themselves – who believed that they already knew everything they needed to know; that their lives were successful, meaningful and fulfilled; and that being a Christian was an easy, straightforward affair that did not require much effort or attention. Because these people possessed so much objective knowledge, they had 'forgotten what it means *to exist*, and what *inwardness* is . . . forgotten what it means to exist religiously'. Such readers would not be able to understand the truth directly; they would not be able to look within themselves clearly, because their view would be distorted by the mistaken image they held of themselves. In *The Point of View for My Work as An Author*, Kierkegaard suggests that it is much more difficult to communicate the truth to those who believe that they already possess it, than to simple, uneducated people who make no claims to knowledge. He uses the metaphor of filling a jar with water to illustrate this point: a simple, unassuming reader is like an empty jar, ready to receive the truth, whereas the reader who is under the illusion of possessing the truth is like a jar that is already full. This jar must be emptied before the truth can be poured in. Indirect communication is the process of emptying the jar, or removing the illusion.

Although this idea that people must become receptive to the truth before they are able to understand it properly is quite unusual within the context of modern philosophy, it is much more familiar within a religious context. Jesus tells a parable about sowing seeds on different types of soil: seeds that fall on hard, unreceptive ground will not be able to grow, whereas seeds that fall on soft, fertile soil will flourish. Likewise, truth will not be appropriated – will not be genuinely learnt – unless the individual's mind is open and ready to receive it. There are many accounts of occasions when religious teachers like Jesus and the Buddha first prepared their listeners, for example by kind words or actions to break down their defences and soften their hearts, before delivering their teachings directly. From a religious point of view, what Kierkegaard calls 'indirect communication' is a tried and tested method for guiding people towards the truth.

Kierkegaard knew that he could not make his readers recognize their illusions simply by pointing these out: 'a direct attack only strengthens a person in his illusion, and at the same time embitters him'. Most people, if accused of being inauthentic, will react defensively and dismiss the accuser, instead of reflecting on themselves. Most people do not react positively to someone who, assuming a position of superiority, preaches at them about their faults. They do not want to listen. No doubt Kierkegaard's imagined reader, if told that he is ignorant and unchristian, would reply indignantly, 'What do you mean? Of course I am a Christian! And I'm one of the most knowledgeable men in Copenhagen! I'm a University Professor'! This reader would assume that the author must be referring to someone else, that these criticisms were not meant for him, and perhaps he would even side with the author in condemning the shallowness and hypocrisy of others. And of course, in any case, Kierkegaard cannot simply accuse all his readers because it is possible that some of them, however educated and sophisticated they may be, are also wise, self-aware and genuinely subjective Christians.

In order to communicate with those readers who *are* deluded, Kierkegaard tries to approach them on their own level, rather than assume a superior stance. He suggests that 'one must approach from behind the person who is under an illusion':

Take the case of a man who is passionately angry, and let us assume that he is really in the wrong. Unless you can begin with him by making it seem that it were he who had to instruct you, and unless you can do it in such a way that the angry man, who was too impatient to listen to a word of yours, is glad to discover in you a complacent and attentive listener – if you cannot do that, you cannot help him at all. Or take the case of a lover who has been unhappy in love, and suppose that the way he yields to his passions is really unreasonable, impious, unchristian. In case you cannot begin with him in such a way that he finds genuine relief in talking to you about his suffering and is able to enrich his mind with the poetical interpretations you suggest for it, notwith-standing you have no share in this passion and want to free him from it – if you cannot do that, then you cannot help him at all; he shuts himself away from you, he retires within himself . . . and then you just talk *at* him.[2]

Kierkegaard claims that most of the so-called Christians he has in mind actually live in 'aesthetic' categories. This means that they do not really engage themselves in life, have a sense of their own inward-ness, fully accept responsibility for themselves, or wholeheartedly commit to anything. The nameless author of the first volume of *Either/Or* is a typical aesthetic personality: he is openly nihilistic, governed by his moods and the pursuit of pleasure, and he plays with abstract ideas without relating them to his own life. However, it is also possible to be outwardly respectable, to have a family and an important job, and to attend church every Sunday, while still having an essentially aesthetic approach to life. The external appearance is meaningless if the individual lacks an inward understanding. Kierkegaard sometimes describes his pseudonymous writings as 'aesthetic' works, because they discuss ideas that 'aesthetic' readers will be interested in, and include characters whom these readers can relate to.

Kierkegaard's communication strategy is nicely illustrated by a biblical story about King David and the prophet Nathan. (Kierkegaard himself explores this story in his religious discourse 'What is Required in Order to Look at Oneself with True Blessing in the Mirror of the Word?', which appears in his book *For Self-Examination*.) According to 2 Samuel 11–12, King David sleeps with Bathsheba while her husband Uriah is away, fighting for David's army. When Bathsheba tells David that she has become pregnant with his child, he recalls Uriah from the battle front and tries to entice him to sleep with his wife – by getting him drunk – in an attempt to cover up his adultery. When this plan fails, David sends Uriah back to fight, instructing his commander to put Uriah in a position where he is sure to be killed. After Uriah's death David marries Bathsheba and she gives birth to a son. God, displeased with David, sends the prophet Nathan to talk to him. Nathan tells the king a parable about a rich man who, although he owns large flocks of sheep, steals and kills his poor neighbour's only lamb to feed an unexpected guest. 'The man who has done this deserves to die!' exclaims David angrily, 'and he should restore the lamb fourfold, because he did this thing, and because he had no pity'. Nathan says to David, 'You are the man'. Realizing fully the wickedness of his actions, David repents of his sin. Kierkegaard's comment on this text illuminates his own writing: 'the tale which the prophet told was a story, but this "You are the man" – this was another story – it was the transition to the subjective'.

In his explicitly religious writings, which take a short biblical text as their point of departure, Kierkegaard treats the scriptures as a mirror in which the reader puts her own subjectivity to the test. Although he does not challenge the orthodox view that the Bible is an authoritative revelation of God, he emphasizes its role in helping the reader to become a Christian. Kierkegaard suggests that many people read the Bible while avoiding looking at themselves in its mirror: they may treat it as a valuable antique, examining the mirror's ornate frame or pointing out cracks in the glass and smudges on its surface. Others will study the Bible historically, trying to determine questions of authorship and authenticity. For Kierkegaard, there is nothing wrong with these pursuits in themselves, but if they are used as a substitute for becoming a Christian then they will be a barrier to salvation. The reader needs to be attentive to the way the Bible addresses her personally: she must receive its words in her heart, and allow them to illuminate her inner being and expose her failings, pretensions and self-deceptions.

This idea that the scriptures hold up a mirror to the reader's true self can be applied to Kierkegaard's writing too – although of course he would insist that, unlike the Bible, his own work has no authority. By creating pseudonyms and other characters with whom readers will empathize and identify, Kierkegaard tricks his readers into seeing themselves more clearly. In *Either/Or*, for example, we are first drawn into the world of the aesthete. The sophisticated reader might find herself assuming the 'objective' perspective of a critic, judging the text's literary and philosophical merits – and this would mirror the aesthete's own attitude. Having identified with the aesthete in this way, readers will feel that Judge William's letters are addressed to them personally. When, at the end of the book, the Judge sends the aesthete a sermon, telling him to 'read this, and think of yourself', this will encourage the reader to use the text for self-reflection. If *Either/Or* consisted only of the Judge's ethical advice, the reader would be less likely to engage with it and to learn from it.

Kierkegaard's 'aesthetic' books that focus most explicitly on Christianity are *Philosophical Fragments* and *Concluding Unscientific Postscript*, both written under the pseudonym Johannes Climacus. Instead of presenting himself as a model Christian and lecturing his readers on all the ways in which they fall short of this ideal, Climacus declares that he is *not* a Christian. This admission would itself be startling to a nineteenth-century reader, but it allows Climacus to discuss the true meaning of Christianity without appearing to talk down to the reader. This in turn allows readers to reflect on the authenticity of their own religious faith, without feeling that they need to defend themselves against an attack. (Kierkegaard himself echoes Climacus's position in a supplementary note to *The Point of View for My Work as An Author*: 'I have never fought in such a way as to say: I am the true Christian, others are not Christians. No, my contention has been this: *I know what Christianity is*, my imperfection as a Christian I myself fully recognize – but I know what Christianity is.')

Kierkegaard uses a similar tactic in *Fear and Trembling*, where the pseudonym Johannes de silentio repeatedly claims that he cannot understand Abraham's willingness to sacrifice his son Isaac. Johannes de silentio writes from the point of view of a philosopher – someone who is familiar with Hegel's philosophy and 'understands it fairly well' – and a well-educated reader with similar philosophical interests would regard him as an equal. When Johannes says that he is unable to understand Abraham, this indicates that the categories of philosophy, and indeed rational thought in general, are inadequate when it comes to making sense of Abraham's religious faith. By identifying with the pseudonym, and being drawn into his attempt to make sense of Abraham's actions, readers may find that they too are unable to understand Abraham. This will force them to see that reason is limited, and cannot grasp the whole of existence.

KIERKEGAARD'S PSEUDONYMS

One of the most unusual and perplexing features of Kierkegaard's writing is his use of pseudonyms – not just a single pseudonym, but several different ones. These pseudonyms have distinct personalities and backgrounds: they are literary characters rather than merely pen-names. We have already seen that Kierkegaard's method of 'indirect communication' uses the pseudonyms to sneak up on readers and surprise them into a recognition of their own existence. This alone does not, however, answer all the questions that are raised by the pseudonymity of the authorship.

An obvious question is whether or not we should regard the pseudonymous texts as expressing Kierkegaard's own views. Kierkegaard himself offers a clear answer to this question in the 'First and Last Explanation' that comes right at the end of the *Concluding Unscientific Postscript*. Unlike the rest of the text, this is written in Kierkegaard's name. After acknowledging that he is the author of eight books and three articles that were published pseudonymously between 1843 and 1846, he states that in these texts 'there is not a single word by me. I have no opinion about them except as a third party, no knowledge of their meaning except as a reader, nor the remotest private relation to them'. Some readers and scholars of Kierkegaard take this declaration literally, and treat the works of different pseudonyms as separate both from one another and from Kierkegaard's signed discourses and later works. Other commentators simply ignore the pseudonyms and treat the ideas presented in the pseudonymous texts as Kierkegaard's own, speaking or writing about 'Kierkegaard's philosophy' as if his status as an author were quite uncontroversial. Both of these positions are rather dubious, and most people take a view somewhere between the two extremes. And as we saw in the last chapter, the question of how far we should identify the pseudonyms with the 'real' Kierkegaard is complicated by the fact that we do not know who this 'real' person was, because it is very difficult to make a clear distinction between Kierkegaard's life and works.

Whatever we think about the connection between Kierkegaard and his pseudonyms, we need to address the question of *why* Kierkegaard wrote in this way. There are several possible reasons to consider, and perhaps a combination of some or all of these comes closest to a satisfactory explanation for the pseudonyms. One theory that we can dismiss, however, is that Kierkegaard wanted to remain unknown. This is certainly not consistent with what we know of his personality – for he was attention-seeking and seemed unafraid of controversy – or with the fact that he published other books under his own name. Moreover, the pseudonyms did not actually cover up Kierkegaard's identity: it soon became common knowledge that he was the author of *Either/Or* and the books that followed, which although written under different names share a distinctive literary style. The 'First and Last Explanation' acknowledges this, and was not written to uncover a secret but to make a statement about Kierkegaard's relationship to his pseudonyms – and in any case, the fact that he makes this statement makes it clear that he did not wish to conceal his identity from the reader.

In 'A First and Last Explanation' Kierkegaard states that the reason for his pseudonymity is to do with the texts themselves – with their communicative purpose – rather than with himself personally: 'my pseudonymity . . . has not had an *accidental* basis in my *person* . . . but an *essential* basis in the *production* itself'. He describes himself as a poet who has created the pseudonyms' names and characters and then merely allowed these characters to speak for themselves. This allows a certain freedom of expression, and enables Kierkegaard to present different views of life without judging them from a moral point of view – and without inviting the moral judgment of his readers. It is acceptable for a fictional character to say things 'which no actual person dares to allow himself or can want to allow himself in the moral limitations of actuality'. Kierkegaard suggests that each pseudonym 'has his definite life-view, and his words, which understood in this way could possibly be meaningful, witty, stimulating, would perhaps sound strange, ludicrous, disgusting in the mouth of a particular factual person'. This also gives the reader more freedom, because she can reflect on the character's views without moral constraints. Perhaps we need to bear in mind here that the amoral attitude expressed by the aesthete in *Either/Or*, particularly in the 'Diary of a Seducer', would have been quite shocking to Kierkegaard's contemporaries, who may have considered it morally wrong to read a book by a real-life writer who lived in such a way and who held such views. Of course, an author could describe this sort of attitude in abstract terms, but the reader will be more deeply affected by a first-person account of this way of life. The pseudonyms, then, allow Kierkegaard to have this kind of impact on the reader without the risk that his books, or he himself, would be considered immoral. Of course, this strategy only works if it is clear that the pseudonym *is* a pseudonym, and not a real person.

This issue of morality, which is the main focus of 'A First and Last Explanation', can only be part of the story, since not all of the pseudonyms are morally reprehensible. Most of them, in fact, seem quite respectable, if somewhat eccentric. As we have seen, the purposes of indirect communication give Kierkegaard other reasons to assume positions that are not necessarily his own. The most important of these positions are that of the philosopher, or abstract thinker, and that of the person who is not a Christian. It is awkward for Kierkegaard himself, who expresses so much contempt for academia and argues that the truth of human existence cannot be grasped through concepts, to produce a work of philosophy. And as we have seen, he attempts to write philosophy in such a way as to expose its limitations, its failure to understand certain aspects of life. He uses pseudonyms such as Johannes de silentio, Johannes Climacus, and Constantin Constantius – the author of *Repetition* – not only to present philosophical ideas, but also to illustrate the struggles involved in being both a philosopher and an existing individual. Constantin Constantius, for example, invents the philosophical concept of 'repetition', which expresses a kind of existential freedom, but because he is limited by his theoretical approach he is unable to practise this concept in his own life. In the end he admits defeat, gives up his inquiry into repetition, and decides to stop philosophizing.

We have already seen how Kierkegaard uses Johannes Climacus's claim that he is not a Christian to communicate with readers who assume that they *are* Christians. Since Kierkegaard was also publishing under his own name 'Edifying Discourses' that are explicitly Christian, he had to use a pseudonym in order to write as a non-Christian author. And in any case, he may not have wanted to claim not to be a Christian for other reasons – because it would damage his reputation, or, more simply, because it would not be true. The pseudonym Anti-Climacus, however, who is the author of *The Sickness Unto Death* and *Practice in Christianity*, has a religious perspective that Kierkegaard regards as more purely Christian than his own:

> Johannes Climacus and Anti-Climacus have several things in common; but the difference is that whereas Johannes Climacus

places himself so low that he even says himself that he is not a Christian, one seems to be able to detect in Anti-Climacus that he considers himself to be a Christian on an extraordinarily high level . . . I would place myself higher than Johannes Climacus, lower than Anti-Climacus.[3]

Kierkegaard recognizes a kind of hierarchy of the pseudonyms, in which he himself, as the author of the 'Edifying Discourses', occupies a middle position. Anti-Climacus is above him, while all the other pseudonyms – who have aesthetic or ethical attitudes to life – are beneath him. Climacus and Anti-Climacus allow Kierkegaard to write about Christianity from contrasting perspectives, both of which he distinguishes from his own.

We should also, however, consider the possibility that the views expressed by the pseudonymous and fictional writers *are* in fact Kierkegaard's own. This gives us quite a different understanding of the pseudonyms. What if they all represent aspects of Kierkegaard himself? Of course, the existential positions of the pseudonyms often oppose or even contradict one another – but individuals do sometimes find within themselves conflicting views and personality traits. Kierkegaard himself was certainly a contradictory character: playful and earnest, forgiving and severe, sociable and reclusive. Why should we expect a philosophical position to be internally consistent, when we are not internally consistent ourselves? Perhaps the texts that portray conflict between two or more pseudonyms represent a conflict within a single person. On this interpretation, a text like *Either/Or* is a way for Kierkegaard thoroughly to examine his shallow, nihilistic, amoral tendencies (and this aesthetic character is not wholly unlikeable), and then to give himself a good ethical talking-to. In *Repetition* there are two characters: the pseudonym Constantin Constantius – an abstract thinker with an interest in modern philosophy – and a nameless young fiancé who has second thoughts about his engagement. These characters are good friends at the beginning of the book, but when the young man finds himself in an ethical crisis he breaks off his contact with Constantin, ceases to ask him for advice, and instead looks to the Book of Job for inspiration. This narrative development reflects a development within an individual who, through a challenging existential situation that reveals to him his own inwardness, realizes the limitations of theoretical reflection and seeks religious guidance. *Repetition* is an extremely enigmatic little book and it is perhaps impossible to produce a definitive interpretation that ties up all its loose ends, but there are hints in the text itself that Constantin Constantius and the fiancé are not in fact two separate people.

Whether we regard the pseudonyms as facets of a single person – whom we may or may not identify with Kierkegaard – or as distinct individuals, it is still the case that they represent different approaches to life. This is certainly one of their key purposes: in his philosophy, Kierkegaard does not want to deal only with abstract ideas, but with existing individuals. The pseudonyms personify various kinds of existence, and these are not just theories or concepts but characters who have histories, who develop, who go through situations and respond to them. This dynamic quality is very important: Kierkegaard criticizes philosophy for its inability to grasp and to articulate the movement, the continual becoming, that characterises existence. His pseudonymous authors discuss philosophical concepts, but they also fall in love, suffer, travel and make decisions. Whereas philosophy is usually concerned with concepts and the relationships between them (and these conceptual relationships were especially emphasized by the Hegelians whom Kierkegaard was most keen to attack), Kierkegaard's thought is concerned with existing individuals and their relationships – to other people, to God and to themselves. He suggests that his pseudonyms offer interpretations of 'the original text of individual human existence-relationships'. Kierkegaard's Christian perspective means that faith and love are central to his philosophy, and these are classes of relationship, not abstract ideas. The pseudonyms may not on the whole exemplify faith and love, but the fact that they struggle with them gives the reader an insight into what these qualities entail.

Kierkegaard was very fond of visiting the theatre, and he often describes his pseudonymous authorship in theatrical terms. His use of fictional characters allows him to dramatize inward existence and to make conflicts play themselves out on the 'stage' of the text. This is a way of animating ideas, of bringing them to life and putting them in motion. It is also a way of engaging the attention of readers and drawing them into the drama. The pseudonyms are not just a novel means of communicating philosophical ideas, but an essential part of Kierkegaard's attempt to create a new, 'existentialist' kind of philosophy.

One final issue that we have to consider in relation to the pseudonyms is that of authority. In the prefaces to his collections of 'Edifying Discourses', Kierkegaard takes care to emphasize that he lacks religious authority: he is not an ordained preacher, and he makes no claim to be a better Christian than any of his readers. He may also have wanted to discourage readers from viewing him as a philosophical authority. This, we can recall, is an important aspect of Socrates' method of 'indirect communication': he wanted people to discover the truth for themselves rather than simply accept it on his authority – and this was not just because he encouraged independent thought, but because the kind of self-knowledge he taught was simply not the kind of truth that could be transmitted from one person to another. Kierkegaard's emphasis on subjective truth as opposed to objective knowledge puts him in a similar position. He wanted to draw his readers' attention to their own subjectivity, their own inwardness, and therefore he felt that he had to 'withdraw Socratically' from them. The pseudonyms help him to do this, partly by acting as a kind of screen (although, as we have seen, their concealing effect was minimal) and partly by creating a multiplicity of perspectives that prevent the reader from identifying a clear, coherent philosophical doctrine or position to latch on to.

We should regard Kierkegaard's claim to share none of his pseudonyms' views as a piece of advice about how to read his books, rather than as a statement of historical fact. He is distancing himself from the pseudonyms in order to discourage us from accepting his books merely on his authority – because we admire him for being cleverer and more learned than ourselves, for example. One of his priorities is to awaken readers to their capacity for choice, and by refusing the role of author and authority-figure he is giving the reader the opportunity to exercise her freedom. Again, we can invoke the title of one of Kierkegaard's signed books to illustrate this point: *Judge for Yourself!* In figuring out our own responses to the different pseudonyms, we reach a clearer sense of what we ourselves believe and value. In this way, as in many others, Kierkegaard's works are very different from other, more conventional philosophical texts, which tend to be written in an authoritative style that includes compelling logical arguments and an impressive vocabulary. The pseudonymous texts exhibit these qualities too – for Kierkegaard certainly wants to persuade us of *something*, and also no doubt to dazzle us with his intellectual prowess – but perhaps the distance that the pseudonyms create between Kierkegaard and his works allowed him to maintain a degree of humility. Pseudonyms offer a certain freedom for the author as well as for the reader: freedom from the need to impress, freedom from the egotistical desire to become a great writer, freedom from the pressure to produce a ground-breaking new philosophy.

WRITING AGAINST PHILOSOPHY

The communicative strategies that we find in Kierkegaard's pseudonymous texts are not only designed to awaken the reader to her own inwardness, but also aim to undermine the traditional project of philosophy. (Actually, these purposes are not completely distinct, because the reader of the pseudonymous works is likely to have an interest in philosophy, whether as a student or as a professional scholar.) Kierkegaard defines the philosophical project as the pursuit of objective knowledge, and he describes his own authorship as 'a polemic against the truth as knowledge'. We will explore this idea in more depth in Chapters 3 and 4, but here we shall examine the way in which Kierkegaard's communicative techniques contribute to his attack on traditional philosophy.

Philosophical method usually consists of logical deduction and rational argument. One of the reasons why Kierkegaard regards this kind of thinking as unsuitable for addressing questions about human existence is that it produces conclusions that are *necessary*. This is a technical term in philosophy, and in this context it means something like unavoidable. To use a popular example, if we accept the propositions (1) that all men are mortal, and (2) that Socrates is a man, then we must also accept the proposition (3) that Socrates is mortal. The point is that, according to the principles of reason, we *must* accept the third proposition, we *have no choice* but to accept it, because it follows as a necessary conclusion from the first two propositions. Because in his own philosophy Kierkegaard addresses questions relating to human freedom, such as how to make choices and decisions, he regards this kind of reasoning as unhelpful from the point of view of the existing individual. This means that he wants to challenge not just a particular philosophical position, but the entire rational method of philosophy itself.

But how does one argue against necessity? How does one oppose what is unavoidable? This highlights another aspect of 'indirect communication': Kierkegaard cannot simply enter directly into a conventional philosophical debate, because he is seeking to transform the terms, the very basis, of this debate. One of his tactics, as we have seen, is to use his pseudonyms and other fictional characters to personify philosophy, and to demonstrate through their experiences the limitations of philosophical method. But these characters are not the only means of indirect communication. Another important strategy is humour, for even the most watertight logical argument can be undermined by making fun of it. Kierkegaard sometimes holds philosophers up for ridicule by caricaturing them as pompous, narrow-minded and foolish, and by making witty and sarcastic comments at their expense. This playfulness is a powerful way to subvert the seriousness and correctness of philosophy. (Reading Kierkegaard is not always, however, an especially amusing pastime. I must confess to occasionally feeling bored and frustrated by his writing. But perhaps even this is a tactic of 'indirect communication': one feels impatient with the first volume of *Either/Or*, for example, because it goes on and on without ever reaching anything satisfactory – does the text deliberately provoke this reaction in order to make a point about the aesthetic way of life?)

Kierkegaard's use of metaphors and recurring motifs is also significant in relation to his 'polemic against the truth as knowledge'. Particularly important in this context are metaphors of movement, which appear very frequently in both the pseudonymous texts and the 'Edifying Discourses'. Kierkegaard regards movement, or becoming, as essential to human existence, and he criticizes philosophy – especially Hegelian philosophy – for attempting to contain this kind of movement within abstract concepts. His pseudonyms and characters who represent the perspective of philosophy often find that they are incapable of movement, or able to move only in a limited way: the aesthete in *Either/Or* complains that 'I feel the way a chessman must, when the opponent says of it: that piece cannot be moved'. Johannes de silentio says that he becomes 'paralysed' when he tries to understand Abraham, and he describes himself as like a person who learns to swim by practising the strokes whilst being suspended in a harness that hangs from the ceiling above the water. In other words, he 'goes through the motions' but doesn't actually go anywhere. In *Repetition* Constantin Constantius paces back and forth in his study, but admits that 'a religious movement I am unable to make, it is contrary to my nature'. Each of these characters exemplifies the limitations of philosophy.

Kierkegaard also uses both characters and metaphors to *show* the movements of existence. One of his most famous metaphors is the 'leap of faith' (actually Kierkegaard does not use this phrase, but he uses the metaphor of a dancer's leap to illustrate the movement of religious faith). This metaphor expresses the way in which faith is a 'double movement': it goes up towards God, but it also comes back down to earth, and this shows that faith is not a withdrawal from the world but a way of living *in* the world through a relationship to God. Abraham's journey to Mount Moriah provides another dynamic metaphor for faith, and in fact this resembles the 'double movement' of the dancer's leap because Abraham walks up the mountain and then comes down again, returning to his home and to his wife Sarah.

Kierkegaard's unusual and indirect communicative techniques aim to undermine philosophical method – but how should we respond to this when we are reading his texts from a philosophical point of view? Does Kierkegaard's style of philosophy leave us powerless to criticize his position, once we have tried to piece together what this position is? Are there criteria other than those of traditional philosophy that we can use to evaluate his thought? Do we as philosophers have to choose between rejecting Kierkegaard, while accepting him as existing individuals? We have not fully addressed the question of communication until we have reflected on our role as readers, without whom the communicative process itself is incomplete.

Usually we evaluate a philosophical text according to the strength, validity, relevance, clarity and thoroughness of its arguments. In doing so, we make certain assumptions about the authority and value of rational thought itself. As we have seen, Kierkegaard wants us to question those assumptions, but it is possible to do this without simply abandoning them. In fact, bringing one's assumptions out into the open and examining them critically has always been an important aspect of philosophical method, and one of the ways in which progress in philosophy comes about. Kierkegaard directs us to look within ourselves for the truth, but it may be that when we do so we find that Hegelian philosophy, or some other rational system, offers the best way to make sense of our own existence. And if this is the case, our self-examination will have served to strengthen for us the authority of rational thought:

we will trust it more deeply when we can relate it to our 'subjective truth'.

Or perhaps we agree with Kierkegaard about the limitations of abstract concepts and philosophical reflection, and are unwilling to apply the usual criteria of rational consistency to his thought. Are there other ways to evaluate his texts? Can we defend them against the rationalist's accusation that they are merely rhetorical and lack coherence? The pseudonymous texts do, in fact, exhibit consistency and coherence, but this is literary or thematic rather than rational or logical. The philosophical views expressed by Kierkegaard's pseudonyms and characters tie in with the metaphors and dramatic developments within his texts, and also with their narrative structure and the ways in which they address the reader. Once we have identified a central theme, such as inwardness or movement, we begin to see that all the elements of a text revolve around it, expressing it in different ways – rather like variations on a musical theme.

Kierkegaard's book *Repetition* provides a particularly good example of this kind of thematic coherence. The centrality of the theme of movement is indicated in the very first sentences of the book, which recall an ancient Greek philosophical debate about motion:

> When the Eleatics [a group of philosophers] denied the possibility of motion, Diogenes, as everyone knows, stepped forward as an opponent. He literally did step forward, for he did not say a word but merely paced back and forth a few times, assuming that in this way he refuted the philosophers.[4]

The text as a whole echoes Diogenes' 'step forward' by using the theme of movement to refute philosophy itself. Whereas the Greek philosophers found that the natural phenomena of motion and change raised metaphysical questions about how something can go from being a certain way to being a different way (is there a moment when it is both at the same time? or when it is neither?), Kierkegaard is interested in the inward, spiritual becoming of the existing individual. It is this kind of movement that he thinks modern philosophy has misunderstood, or overlooked altogether. The pseudonym Constantin Constantius criticizes Hegel's concept of movement, known as 'mediation', and suggests that the Greek philosophers – particularly Aristotle – had a superior understanding of motion. He puts forward his own theory about existential movement, based on the concept of repetition: it is through the continual repetition of the moment of choice that the individual exercises her freedom and becomes herself. Constantin Constantius tests his theory of repetition by travelling to Berlin, where he has previously spent an enjoyable holiday, and attempting to repeat the experience. He stays at the same hotel, sees the same play at the same theatre, eats in the same restaurant – but each time he is disappointed, and he fails to achieve a repetition. He has missed the point that repetition is an inward movement, not an external one. The young fiancé, on the other hand, develops inwardly but spends several weeks physically immobile: 'I am inside . . . I do not stir from the spot . . . All I know is that I am standing and have been standing *suspenso gradu* [immobilized] for a whole month now, without moving a foot or making a single movement.' In this text, then, we find metaphors, philosophical discussions, anecdotes and a narrative structure that all converge on the theme of movement, and this gives the book an internal coherence and consistency even though it does not present a rational argument for its position.

Kierkegaard's use of 'indirect communication' in the pseudonymous texts means that the reader faces a task of interpretation as well as a task of comprehension and analysis. Most philosophical texts are challenging, but these present a double challenge: first we have to work out what Kierkegaard is trying to say, before we can reflect on and respond to it. Although this particular kind of complexity is unique to Kierkegaard's authorship, it encourages us to consider the question of communication – and especially our own role as readers – in a way that is useful for approaching other philosophical texts. There are many different ways of reading a text, and becoming aware of this enables us to deepen our understanding. Kierkegaard knew that contemporary readers of his explicitly philosophical books would have certain kinds of expectations: to increase their knowledge, to stimulate their intellects, to criticize, to keep up with a fashion in the literary world. We may now add to this list: to study for or to teach a university course, to produce a PhD thesis, to write a book about Kierkegaard. Do these approaches conflict with the movement of inward reflection that all Kierkegaard's texts, pseudonymous and overtly religious, prompt us to make? Or is there a way of reading that stays faithful to both intellectual and personal interests? Is it really so difficult to be a philosopher and an existing individual *at the same time*? I cannot answer these questions for you, and probably Kierkegaard can't either. The final words of *Either/Or* here seem very apt:

> Ask yourself, and keep on asking yourself until you find the answer, for one can recognise a thing a thousand times and acknowledge it, one can want a thing many times and attempt it, yet only the deep inner movement, only the indescribable emotions of the heart, only these convince you that what you have recognised *belongs to you*, that no power can take it from you; for only the truth that edifies [changes you for the better] is the truth for you.

CHAPTER 3

KIERKEGAARD'S CRITIQUE OF HEGEL

HEGEL'S PHILOSOPHY: RATIONALISM, HISTORY, RECONCILIATION

When reading a philosophical text, it is always important to consider its historical context. Philosophy is an historical phenomenon: we can trace the Western philosophical tradition back to ancient Greece, where people began to construct theories to make sense of the world and to work out how best to live in it. Much of this philosophizing was – as it still is today – oral, consisting of conversation and debate, but some thinkers wrote down their ideas and this practice of recording philosophical reflections created what we now recognize as the philosophical tradition. This tradition is like an ongoing dialogue: philosophers write in response to the ideas of previous philosophers, sometimes defending or developing them, and sometimes arguing that they are inadequate and suggesting alternatives. A critique of a particular philosophy may take the form of proposing a different solution to a classic problem, or it may involve approaching the problem in a completely new way or even showing that the problem itself is misleading. Philosophy is by its very nature critical, since the practice of philosophy involves a refusal to take things at face value; on the other hand, though, the work of past philosophers always provides a starting-point. Even the most original, creative thinkers draw on methods and concepts from the philosophical tradition. Of course, philosophers also respond to new scientific developments and to the social and political environment of their time, and so the tradition absorbs these external influences as well as developing within itself.

In order to understand Kierkegaard's philosophy, then, we have to have some grasp of what he is responding to. The most important influence on Kierkegaard's thought is the German philosopher Georg Wilhelm Friedrich Hegel, who published extremely influential work from the beginning of the nineteenth century until his death in 1831 (when Kierkegaard was eighteen years old). Hegel's contribution to philosophy was not simply another interpretation of the world and of human life, but a whole new method of philosophizing: he created a system of logic that broke with the traditional model of thought, which had remained more or less unchallenged since the time of Aristotle. Some of Kierkegaard's teachers at the University of Copenhagen were very keen on Hegel's ideas, and more generally the Hegelian approach to philosophical thinking had a great impact on the intellectual culture within which Kierkegaard developed his own philosophy.

Kierkegaard's attitude to Hegel is ambivalent. His thought owes a great deal to Hegelian philosophy, and in his journals he expresses his admiration for Hegel:

> I feel what for me at times is an enigmatic respect for Hegel; I have learned much from him, and I know very well that I can still learn much more from him when I return to him again . . . His philosophical knowledge, his amazing learning, the insight of his genius, and everything else good that can be said of a philosopher I am willing to acknowledge as any disciple.[1]

However, Kierkegaard's published writings continually seek to undermine and discredit Hegelian thought. He is particularly critical of the interpretation of Christianity presented by Hegel and his followers, and in many ways his own account of what it means to live a Christian life is motivated by a conviction that Hegel's view of Christianity is misguided, and even spiritually damaging.

Understanding the influence of Hegel on Kierkegaard's thought is by no means easy, for several reasons. Given Hegel's importance for Kierkegaard, it would seem sensible to read his major works before tackling Kierkegaard's authorship – but Hegel's texts are amongst the most difficult of all philosophical literature. Although his ideas are exciting and compelling, his style of writing tends to be heavy and rather abstract. In fact, there is little evidence that Kierkegaard himself read much, if any, of Hegel's work. His knowledge of Hegel was largely secondhand – at best: as a student he attended some lectures on Hegelian philosophy, but he often skipped these and instead copied the notes of other, more conscientious students. This may seem fortunate for us insofar as it suggests that, in order to read Kierkegaard, we need not be any better acquainted with Hegel's texts than he was himself. But it raises questions about how to interpret Kierkegaard's critique of Hegel: the fact that this critique is not based on a detailed examination of primary texts makes it difficult to evaluate. How well did Kierkegaard understand Hegel's philosophy? Does he misrepresent it, and if so does this undermine his own position? What are the differences between Kierkegaard's idea of Hegel and the 'real' Hegel?

Kierkegaard's encounter with Hegel was mediated by the Danish Hegelians who propagated their mentor's philosophy. When he attacks 'Hegel' his target is a kind of amalgam of Hegel's own ideas and their presentation by these Danish teachers and writers. More than this, however, Kierkegaard tends to conflate Hegelian philosophy with academic life in general. He regards Hegel's work, which emphasizes that conceptual thinking is the very highest expression of the human spirit, as absolutely typical of a narrowly intellectual approach to existence. As we saw in Chapter 1, Kierkegaard's own experience of academia was not particularly positive: he found some of his professors to be pretentious and superficial, and even though he loved ideas he often felt trapped within intellectual reflection, unable to get beyond abstract possibilities and actually put them into practice. So all mixed up in Kierkegaard's critique of Hegel is hostility to certain Hegelian teachers whom he disliked personally or considered intellectually inferior to himself; dissatisfaction with academic life in general; and an ambivalent attitude towards his own highly reflective character.

The issue is complicated still further by the way Kierkegaard expresses his opposition to Hegelian philosophy. As we have seen, Kierkegaard's style of communication is often indirect, and his attack on Hegel is neither straightforward nor explicit. Often he does not discuss Hegel directly, but uses typical Hegelian vocabulary sarcastically or contemptuously: when he mentions 'speculative philosophy', 'the system', 'the Idea' or 'mediation', contemporary readers would have been well aware that these phrases refer to Hegelian philosophy. He does not set out Hegel's position and argue against it point for point; because Hegelian thought is extremely systematic, Kierkegaard expresses his opposition by being deliberately unsystematic. Instead of arguing against Hegel on his terms, Kierkegaard uses the literary techniques of pseudonyms, character, metaphor and narrative to produce a dramatized conflict between Hegelian thought and the perspective of the existing individual. In this way he attempts to show that Hegel's philosophical system misses important truths relating to human existence as it is experienced from a subjective point of view. For example, in *Fear and Trembling* the pseudonym Johannes de silentio claims that although he understands Hegelian philosophy fairly well, he is unable to understand Abraham's religious faith, and this is supposed to demonstrate that Hegel's perspective is inadequate when it comes to making sense of the individual's personal relationship to God.

In order to gain a clearer appreciation of Kierkegaard's complex and ambiguous relationship to Hegel, we have to work through the different layers of this relationship, beginning with Hegel himself, and then moving on to the interpretations of Hegelian philosophy that Kierkegaard encountered as a student in Copenhagen. During the 1830s, when Kierkegaard was studying philosophy and theology at university, Danish Hegelians were engaged in debates with other intellectuals who rejected Hegel's ideas, and this discussion became a matter of more than academic interest when it focused on the religious issues surrounding Hegel's new system of logic. When we look at these debates it becomes clear that Kierkegaard's philosophy developed in response to them, and this provides a context that sheds much light on his authorship.

First, then, some of the key aspects of Hegel's philosophy. There are three Hegelian themes that are particularly relevant from the point of view of Kierkegaard's critique: rationalism, history, and the idea of unity or reconciliation. Rationalism is a philosophical position that recognizes reason as the highest authority in the pursuit of truth, and in the attempt to live a good human life. A rationalist will accept other sources of knowledge, such as evidence provided by the senses, intuition, traditional wisdom, sacred texts, the laws of the state, or dogmatic religious teachings, only if these stand up to the scrutiny of reason. Although most Western philosophers have recognized rational thought as an essential tool, it was not until the seventeenth century – beginning with Descartes – that reason was viewed as independent from, and accorded higher authority than, Christian doctrine. Rationalism became especially predominant in the Enlightenment period, which was characterized by great confidence in the power of human reason to achieve intellectual and technological progress, and to provide the basis for a social structure that combined equality, order and freedom.

Hegel, writing in the early decades of the nineteenth century, represents the culmination of Enlightenment thinking. His work responds primarily to the philosophy of Immanuel Kant, a pivotal thinker of the Enlightenment. Kant's rationalism aims to secure the authority of reason by confining it within its proper limits. Kant offers a thorough critique of the human capacity for understanding, and draws a clear distinction between what can be known and what lies beyond knowledge. He argues that the nature of reality, considered independently from our experience, can never be accessible to our understanding, since our knowledge of the world is shaped by the processes of perception that are common to all human minds. We cannot step outside our minds to encounter something that is independent of ourselves: we can *only* experience reality on *our* terms. For Kant there is an unbridgeable gulf between our human perspective and objective reality: we can never be sure that the way things appear to us corresponds to how they actually are in themselves. Hegel argues against Kant that this division between the subjective and objective standpoints, and between appearances and reality, is only a stage in the process of rational understanding, and can be overcome.

Hegel's deep insight is that we are not separate from reality but a part of it: reality is an outside-less whole that encompasses everything, including the human capacity for rational reflection. In fact, human reason enables reality to know itself, to become transparent to itself. To illustrate this idea it is useful to consider the example of language, which is perhaps less abstract than the notion of reason. We might suppose that language is something separate and secondary that *applies to* the world, but if we regard language as *part of* the world then we can say that through language the world expresses and describes itself. For Hegel, subjectivity and objectivity are not two distinct things, but aspects of a single whole: if they appear to be separate, it is the task of reason to bring to light the relationship between them.

Hegel understands reason as the basic principle which explains all of reality. Unlike Kant, he does not regard reason as a capacity belonging only to human beings: reason simply is the logic of reality, the way the world works, in both its natural and its spiritual dimensions. On this view, whatever is real is rational, and whatever is rational must be real. However, this truth is not fully explicit: some aspects of reality – indeed, some aspects of ourselves – seem to be opaque and mysterious. According to Hegel, this is not because they are irrational or inaccessible to knowledge, but because the unity of reason and reality has not yet, in these cases, been recognized. Although reality is rational and therefore knowable, this does not mean that it has in fact been known: reason is a *process* through which the logic of reality becomes increasingly clear and explicit. The goal of this process is reason's complete recognition and expression of itself as the whole of reality. Hegel suggests that the task of philosophy is to explain the progress of reason towards this goal.

In his philosophy, Hegel distinguishes between the structure or concept of reason – that is, the way it works – and the actual process of reason as it develops through history. He explains the concept of reason in his *Science of Logic*, which shows how thinking moves from one idea to its opposite and then to an understanding of the relationship between the two. For example, the idea of *being* applies to everything except *non-being*; non-being seems to be opposed to and excluded from being; but then we see that there is a relationship or transition between them, which is *becoming*. This may appear rather abstract, but the main point of Hegel's logic is that contradiction is the starting-point for a dynamic connection between the two opposing terms, which are each understood more fully once they are seen in relationship to one another. The concepts of being and non-being are not independent, but parts of a larger idea which includes not just both concepts but also the distinction *and* the relationship between them.

Hegel describes this dynamic relationship as 'mediation', and according to his philosophy it is the basic principle of reason. Hegel's system of logic is quite different from Aristotelian logic, which is based on the assumption that the contradiction between 'A' and 'not-A' (for example, being and non-being) is irreconcilable. Aristotle insists that it is impossible to assert both 'A' and 'not-A', and that one has to assert either one or the other; these basic rules of logic have become known as the *principle of contradiction* and the *law of the excluded middle*. From this point of view, contradiction represents a kind of impasse: there is no middle way between two opposites, and for Aristotle these logical boundaries make definitions, concepts and meanings possible. However, Hegel challenges the Aristotelian laws of logic in order to create a dynamic system of thought. He argues that reality as a whole is never static, and that therefore if reason is to grasp the truth of reality then it must also be capable of movement and development.

The actual process through which reason – the structure of reality – makes itself increasingly clear and explicit is described in other texts, such as the *Philosophy of Nature*, the *Philosophy of Spirit*, and the *Phenomenology of Spirit*. These works present a comprehensive system of natural, psychological, social, artistic and religious forms of reality as they have developed through history. One of Hegel's most influential ideas is that particular individuals and events can be understood as products of historical processes, and this means that an understanding of history is essential to the pursuit of knowledge. Hegel always emphasizes the interactions between different aspects of reality, and he suggests that the progress of history can be rationalized according to the logical principle of mediation. His interpretation of Christianity illustrates this, and of course this is a particularly relevant example in the context of Kierkegaard's critique. Hegel suggests that Jewish spirituality is characterized by a division between God and man, and he regards the incarnation of God in the human form of Jesus Christ as a kind of mediation or reconciliation that overcomes this division. Jesus, and later the social institution of the Church, mediate between human beings and God. For Hegel, the pattern of mediation is also revealed in the doctrine of the Trinity, which teaches that God is Father, Son and Holy Spirit: Father and Son are distinct, but are united by the Spirit, whose essence is love.

Hegel shows that truth is not static and eternal, but dynamic and historical. He recognizes that different societies in different eras have fundamentally different values and ways of life, and that truth has to be understood as relative to these contexts. He also recognizes that truth can be expressed in different ways – for example, works of art, religious teachings, or philosophical systems. Artists convey truth through material form; religion presents the truth symbolically; and philosophy articulates truth by means of concepts. True to his own historical era of Enlightenment rationalism, Hegel argues that concepts are the most direct and transparent medium for expressing truth, and he suggests that philosophy offers a more complete and satisfactory account of reality than religion or art. Of course, art, religion and philosophy are all *aspects of* reality as well as ways of expressing insight into it, and this means that a philosophical system should include an account of art, religion, and philosophy itself and of their histories. Hegel tries to translate the truths expressed in important works of art and in religious doctrines – particularly Christian theology – into conceptual terms. Of course, we must remember that for Hegel concepts are not separate from but intrinsic to the real world: philosophy articulates the *self-explication* of reality as a whole.

HEGELIAN PHILOSOPHY IN DENMARK

In the 1830s, when Kierkegaard was studying at the University of Copenhagen, Hegel's philosophy was fresh, exciting and controversial. Some philosophers and theologians embraced the new system of thought, while others who rejected it tended to defend traditional Aristotelian logic against the Hegelian emphasis on the historicality of truth, and against the idea of mediation. In other words, debate about Hegel's philosophy often took the form of a conflict between Hegelian and Aristotelian systems of logic – between the principles of mediation and contradiction.

In Copenhagen the most influential supporters of Hegelian philosophy were Johan Heiberg, a poet, playwright and literary critic, and Hans Martensen, a prominent theologian. In the early 1830s Heiberg delivered and published lectures on Hegel's logic, and in 1837 he started an academic journal called *Perseus*, which was devoted to discussion of Hegelian ideas. This journal encouraged the debates about logic that, as we shall see, were to influence Kierkegaard's writing of the 1840s. For example, in 1837 a philosophy professor called F.C. Sibbern, who was one of Kierkegaard's teachers, published an article criticizing *Perseus*, attacking Hegel's principle of mediation, and defending Aristotelian logic.

Martensen was a close friend of Heiberg, and he also taught Hegel's philosophy at the University of Copenhagen. In 1839 one of Martensen's graduate students unintentionally prompted a fierce debate when he published an article in which he suggested that 'in theology both rationalism and supernaturalism are antiquated standpoints that belong to a time that has disappeared'. This rather sweeping statement implies that the distinction between rationalism and supernaturalism – which are two alternative approaches to religious belief – can be overcome through Hegelian mediation.

Bishop Mynster, an important and well-respected figure within the Danish Church, was provoked by this comment into writing an article entitled 'Rationalism, Supernaturalism', which draws a clear distinction between these two positions and argues that contemporary Christian believers have to choose to commit to one or the other. Mynster ends his article by appealing to Aristotle's law of the excluded middle (either 'A' or 'not-A'; either rationalism or supernaturalism) in support of his claim that the contradiction between the two positions cannot be overcome.

Heiberg then responded with an article that defended Hegelian philosophy against the criticisms of both Mynster and Sibbern. This was followed by an article by Martensen, who echoed Heiberg's defence of Hegel but focused more on the implications of the principle of mediation for Christian doctrine. Martensen's article, entitled 'Rationalism, Supernaturalism and the Principle of the Excluded Middle', suggests that the contrast between Aristotelian and Hegelian logic reflects the contrast between Judaism and Christianity. Martensen claims that the Jewish faith is characterized by a division between man and God that cannot be reconciled, and that the Jews' refusal to accept Jesus as the son of God rests on the Aristotelian assumption that two contradictory terms – in this case, the divine and human natures – cannot be combined in a single individual. The Christian doctrine of the Incarnation, on the other hand, expresses the truth of the principle of mediation, showing 'that Christian metaphysics cannot remain in an either/or, but that it must find its truth in the third which [Aristotle's law of the excluded middle] excludes'. Martensen also emphasizes that the Jewish God is transcendent, beyond the world, whereas the Christian God has become part of human reality and is now immanent to, or within, the world. The task of modern theology, he suggests, is to clarify God's immanence in conceptual terms, for example by showing that the meaning of the doctrine of the Trinity is 'the key to the entire system of the world'.

Martensen's philosophical interpretation of the differences between Christianity and Judaism implies that Hegelian mediation represents a progression in spiritual understanding, enabling religious thought to reach a more complete truth than could be grasped within the laws of Aristotelian logic. Several times in his article Martensen uses the phrase 'either/or', which in this context refers to Aristotle's principle of contradiction and law of the excluded middle, and to Mynster's insistence on the irreconcilable opposition between rationalism and supernaturalism. As a Hegelian, Martensen wants to move beyond Aristotelian logic, and to show that contradiction can lead to mediation: 'is it not the task of our age to overcome this disastrous either/or?'

In 1842 Bishop Mynster stepped back into the debate, criticizing Martensen's Hegelian theology in an article on contemporary interpretations of Aristotelian logic. Mynster uses the principle of contradiction and the law of the excluded middle to clarify those beliefs that belong to true Christianity and those that must remain outside it. He argues that rationalism and supernaturalism and – more fundamentally – theism (belief in God) and atheism, are contradictory positions: 'the completely contradictory opposite of theism is atheism . . . Supernaturalism must always have rationalism outside itself, and vice versa . . . In respect to the characteristic thing in both points of view, by which they have received their names in the language, the law of exclusion is valid; either/or: there is no third'. The difference between the positions cannot be overcome, and this means that the individual has to choose one or the other: theism or atheism, and, if theism, rationalism or supernaturalism.

Mynster concedes that the idea of mediation can in a way be applied to Christian doctrine, but his views on this matter are not based on enthusiasm for Hegelian philosophy. He certainly disagrees with Martensen's claim that the Christian God is immanent within the world, as opposed to transcendent. Instead, he argues that God always has been, and always will be, both beyond and above the world and omnipotent throughout it. Whereas Martensen suggested that in Judaism God is completely distinct from the world, Mynster uses quotations from the Hebrew scriptures to highlight examples of God's presence within the world: 'Am I a God afar off, and not a God close at hand? Do I not fill heaven and earth?' (Jeremiah 23.23). Mynster argues that immanence is an important aspect of both the Jewish and the Christian understanding of God, because these religions emphasize that God is involved in the world and particularly in human concerns. However, they also insist that God is transcendent, elevated above and separate from the world. Without this insistence on transcendence, suggests Mynster, these religions could not be considered genuinely theistic.

Although Mynster engages seriously with the philosophical and logical issues related to his debate with Martensen, he makes it clear that it is his religious beliefs that provide the foundation for his thinking. His attitude to philosophy is quite different from the Hegelian view that philosophy provides the highest and most complete expression of the truth. Mynster accepts that philosophy raises interesting questions and offers thought-provoking insights, but he does not think that Christianity needs philosophical support or justification for the truths expressed in the Bible. In other words, he rejects the project of Enlightenment rationalism. Mynster suggests that the most important truth is the kind that an individual can exist within, and live her live in accordance with, and he states that *he* finds this truth in Christianity rather than in any philosophical system. He presents faith and philosophy as two alternative perspectives, and rejects the Hegelian attempt to reach a standpoint from which it can understand reality as a whole. As a Christian, he approaches God 'from below', with humility and awe. Mynster sees this as essential to Christian faith: 'That I cannot go in for [the Hegelian] point of view is not due to the fact that I am prejudiced or out-of-date in now old-fashioned systems . . . For my part I must abandon the hope of being able to "look down from above"; but . . . the consolation that comforts me [is] that also from below one can see the highest, and when one keeps that in mind, one ascends towards it.' This suggests that Hegelian philosophy does not allow room for the individual to 'ascend towards' God, because it tries to assume for itself God's omniscient perspective. Mynster's emphasis is on the individual's personal relationship to God, and he is more interested in spiritual progress within this relationship than in the Hegelian idea of reason's progression towards full comprehension of reality as a whole.

The debate between Mynster, Martensen, Heiberg and other academics in Copenhagen provides an illuminating background to Kierkegaard's authorship. Particularly significant is the way the phrase 'either/or' is used in this context to refer to Aristotelian logic: the fact that Kierkegaard called his first major work *Either/Or* indicates that it responds to the debate about Hegelian philosophy. Given Martensen's view that it was 'the task of the age to overcome the disastrous either/or', Kierkegaard's title suggests a defiant assertion of its importance, and this implies an attack on Hegelian logic. Contemporary readers, especially those who had followed the debate between Mynster and Martensen, would have understood straight away that *Either/Or* was concerned with the issues of mediation and contradiction.

EITHER/OR: KIERKEGAARD'S CRITIQUE OF HEGEL

Kierkegaard's choice of the title *Either/Or* indicates that the ideas in this book were shaped by the recent philosophical and theological debates about Hegelian and Aristotelian logic. However, Kierkegaard's intellectual development during the 1830s was influenced as much by his disenchantment with academia as by the various philosophies he encountered within it. He did not want to be an academic philosopher, and he was contemptuous of the concept of professional thinker. This is one of the reasons why his books are written in such an unusual style: Kierkegaard did not just want to produce another theory or system, but to put the practice of philosophy as a whole into question.

In a sense *Either/Or* contributes to the debate about mediation and contradiction, but this text is very different in both style and content from the articles that had been written by Mynster and Martensen. Instead of arguing that one kind of logic is better than another, Kierkegaard shows what kind of life a person would live if it were based on the Hegelian principle of mediation, or on the Aristotelian principle of contradiction. By dramatizing the philosophical debates of his contemporaries, he takes the issues out of a purely reflective, theoretical context, and into actual existence. There is in Kierkegaard's thought an attempt to move beyond academic philosophy, as well as to criticize Hegelian ideas in particular. This means that his relationship to both the philosophical tradition and the academic world is rather ambiguous: on the one hand he draws from concepts created by other philosophers, which were already topical – such as Aristotle's principle of contradiction – but on the other hand he uses these concepts to argue that philosophy cannot express the whole truth about human existence.

Either/Or is divided into two parts, each written by a different character, and readers usually assume that the title refers to the alternatives of *either* the aesthetic approach to life presented in volume 1, *or* the ethical attitude recommended by Judge William in volume 2. To some extent this is true, but it is not the whole story. As we have seen, 'either/or' signifies the Aristotelian principle of contradiction, and this is an important issue within both parts of the book. As Bishop Mynster had already argued, insisting on 'either/or' means that the individual is faced with a choice between two alternatives, and it is this issue of choice that distinguishes between the aesthetic and the ethical lifestyles. The aesthete is unwilling to choose or commit to anything, whereas Judge William repeatedly emphasizes that it is important to make a decision about the kind of person one wants to be. In his letters to the aesthete he argues that 'as a free spirit I am born of the principle of contradiction, or born by the fact that I choose myself'.

For Judge William, exercising choices is the most essential aspect of ethical life, for it is this that makes a person responsible for herself. He regards freedom not as a state lacking all restraints, but as an ability to take active responsibility for one's life. Judge William argues that it is possible to make a meaningful choice only if there is a genuine and irreconcilable difference between alternative possibilities. It certainly seems that the nature of finite existence means that choices have to be made: at any particular moment in time, one can either be speaking or silent, indoors or outdoors, married or unmarried – but one cannot be both at once. Judge William presents this idea as a practical application of Aristotle's logical principle of contradiction: 'that which is prominent in my either/or is the ethical . . . It is a question of the reality of the act of choice.'[2]

Rather like Bishop Mynster, Judge William uses the principle of contradiction to criticize Hegelian philosophy. However, his approach is very different, as he does not emphasize the distinction between particular beliefs, but instead focuses on the idea that freedom must be based on 'either/or'. (The 'Ultimatum' at the end of *Either/Or* emphasizes the importance of freedom in the context of the religious individual's relationship to God.) Judge William argues that Hegel's logic of mediation might apply to concepts, but not to life as it is experienced from the perspective of the existing individual:

If we concede mediation, then there is no absolute choice . . . then there is no absolute either/or. This is the difficulty, yet I believe that it is due partly to the fact that two spheres are confounded with one another: that of thought and that of freedom. The opposition does not remain for thought, which goes over to the other side and thereupon combines both [concepts] in a higher unity. For freedom the opposition does remain, for freedom excludes the other side.[3]

Judge William also emphasizes that ethical life is concerned with the future: with making decisions about what to do, and trying to become a particular kind of person. He suggests that when mediation attempts to explain actual events, it can only cope with the past, with things that have already happened. History might be rationalized in retrospect, but life has to be lived forwards – and indeed, people in the past were living their lives forwards too, and so in a sense the logic of mediation does not account for their freedom. When history was actually happening, at every moment it contained an 'either/or'. (This idea is developed further in *Philosophical Fragments*, where the pseudonym Johannes Climacus argues that everything historical has come into existence freely, criticizing the Hegelian view that the past can be understood as a logical process.) Judge William suggests that the philosopher is like 'an antiquarian', only interested in the past, and Hegel, who places so much emphasis on history, is clearly his main target here:

> The philosopher says, 'That's the way it has been hitherto'. I ask, 'What am I to do if I do not want to become a philosopher?' For if I want to do that, I see clearly enough that I, like the other philosophers, shall soon get to the point of mediating the past . . . There is no answer to my question of what I ought to do; for if I was the most gifted philosophical mind that ever lived in the world, there must be one more thing I have to do besides sitting and contemplating the past.[4]

There is of course a certain irony here: this comment is quite typical of the way Kierkegaard simultaneously participates in, and distances himself from, the practice of philosophy. Even while he – or, in this case, Judge William – is criticizing philosophy, he is making a philosophical point about the individual's relationship to the past and the future, and raising the question of how to think in an ethical context.

Judge William's discussion of the importance of 'either/or' is not merely theoretical: he is addressing the aesthete personally and giving him earnest advice about his life. To some extent the aesthete personifies Hegelian philosophy, insofar as he is incapable of facing the future, making choices and realizing his freedom. In other words, the aesthetic approach to existence is characterized by a denial of 'either/or'. Judge William observes that the aesthete's attitude

> Bears a strange resemblance to the pet theory of the newer philosophy, that the principle of contradiction is annulled . . . You

mediate contradictions in a higher madness, philosophy mediates them in a higher unity . . . At this point you are united with the philosophers. What unites you is that life comes to a stop.[5]

Here Kierkegaard, through Judge William, is making a point that is central to his critique of Hegel, and that appears in many other forms elsewhere in his work: he is claiming that there is no movement in Hegelian philosophy. As we have seen, Hegel emphasizes the dynamic quality of reality, and attempts to construct a system of thought that reflects this: mediation is a *process* through which the truth is realized. Kierkegaard, however, argues that the kind of movement that is most important from the point of view of the existing individual involves exercising freedom. He is interested in the task of becoming a self – and more particularly 'the task of becoming a Christian' – and he finds that Hegelian philosophy, with its emphasis on concepts and the use of reason, cannot do justice to this existential movement.

Judge William's direct remarks about the inadequacies of mediation are just one aspect of the critique of Hegelian thought that is presented in *Either/Or*. The fact that the aesthete in some way represents the principle of mediation implies that his shortcomings are shared by Hegelian philosophy. The aesthete is amoral and nihilistic, unwilling to recognize value or purpose in life. He entertains countless possibilities but is unable to choose any of them – he can only remain indifferent. In a section headed 'Either/or: an ecstatic lecture', the aesthete expresses this attitude of indifference:

> If you marry, you will regret it; if you do not marry, you will also regret it . . . Laugh at the world's follies, you will regret it; weep over them you will also regret that . . . Believe a woman, you will regret it, believe her not, you will also regret that . . . Hang yourself, you will regret it; do not hang yourself, and you will also regret that; hang yourself or do not hang yourself, you will regret both . . . This, gentlemen, is the sum and substance of all philosophy.[6]

(It is worth remembering that the aesthete's attitude would have been more shocking to nineteenth-century readers than it is today, when we are more used to this point of view.) Kierkegaard is suggesting that this nihilistic indifference would be the effect of mediation if it were adopted as a principle to live by. 'Life is so empty and meaningless', complains the aesthete, 'how barren is my soul . . . always before me an empty space'. He describes a kind of inward, existential paralysis, comparing himself to a chess piece that cannot be moved. He is melancholy and spiritually impotent, unable to develop and realize his human potential: 'Time flows, life is a stream, people say, and so on. I do not notice it. Time stands still, and I with it.'[7]

By highlighting the parallels between the aesthetic way of life and Hegel's philosophy, Kierkegaard undermines the Hegelian attempt to incorporate the whole of reality into a system of thought. Even though this system claims to include ethics and religion, it remains confined to the aesthetic level of existence, which lacks the freedom that ethical and religious life requires. Kierkegaard suggests that Hegelian philosophy, like the aesthete, is stuck in the sphere of reflection and cannot transform ideas, or possibilities, into actuality. This critique of Hegel is developed in later texts, but examining the way *Either/Or* deals with the issues of mediation and contradiction highlights the way in which Kierkegaard's work aims to respond to, but also to move beyond, previous academic debates about these ideas.

Either/Or focuses on the theme of contradiction in order to explore the nature of freedom from the point of view of the existing individual. Judge William argues that becoming a particular kind of person means making choices and committing to or repeating them. Broadly speaking, ethical life can be defined in terms of understanding one's freedom, and taking responsibility for it by engaging seriously with the question of how best to use it. Implicit in this text is the suggestion that Hegelian philosophy, like the aesthete, falls short of this basic ethical demand. (Elsewhere Kierkegaard complains, quite wrongly, that Hegelian philosophy does not even include an ethics.)

In later texts, particularly those under the pseudonym Johannes Climacus, the idea of contradiction is used in a different context: the theological doctrine of the Incarnation. Here again the emphasis on contradiction stands opposed to the Hegelian idea of mediation. In *Philosophical Fragments* and *Concluding Unscientific Postscript*, Climacus insists that the contradiction between being God and man is absolute: we might say that these alternatives constitute an 'either/or'. While Hegel regards the Christian teaching that Jesus is both human and divine as a case of mediation, Kierkegaard's pseudonym insists that if these two contradictory natures really do exist in the same individual, then this is a paradox – a self-contradictory idea that the understanding simply cannot grasp. To claim that the Incarnation signifies mediation is to show how it is transparent to reason, whereas describing it as a paradox suggests that it cannot be rationalized. In fact, this leaves the individual with a choice – and here we return to Kierkegaard's first interpretation of 'either/or' – between accepting and rejecting the doctrine of the incarnation. The paradox cannot be accepted on rational grounds, but if reason is prepared to step aside, to surrender itself, then the individual can have faith in the reality of something that lies beyond her intellectual capacity. On this view, the event of the Incarnation *does* bring man closer to God, but not through mediation. Instead, it makes a demand for faith that the individual can freely respond to.

One important aim of Kierkegaard's critique of Hegel is to undermine the subordination of religion to philosophy, of faith to reason, within the Hegelian system, and to offer an alternative hierarchy. Kierkegaard's hierarchy is not between different forms of cultural life, but between different ways of existing, or different possible subjectivities. His three main categories are, in ascending order, the aesthetic, the ethical and the religious, although there are further variations within each of these. We will look at these forms of existence in more detail in the next chapter, and then again when we come to discuss *Fear and Trembling*; here we will merely note that Kierkegaard includes the practice of philosophy within the lowest, aesthetic sphere. This happens in *Either/Or*, where Judge William draws attention to the similarities between the aesthete's way of life and Hegelian philosophy; at times he extends the comparison to philosophy in general. Right through Kierkegaard's authorship there runs the claim that, from an existential point of view, intellectual reflection alone is unable to reach the goals of ethical and religious life. Religious faith is presented as a greater task and a rarer achievement than rational thought.

It is difficult to imagine the shape and direction of Kierkegaard's philosophy without the influence of Hegel, both positively and negatively. The figure of Hegel, often caricatured and perhaps misrepresented, is present within all of Kierkegaard's texts, even if he is not mentioned explicitly. Kierkegaard's insistence that truth should be understood in terms of a movement of becoming is inspired by Hegel, even though this idea is used to undermine Hegelian philosophy. His attempt to shift the focus of philosophical thinking from objective truth to the perspective of the existing individual is also a response to Hegel: whereas Hegel argues that individuals find fulfilment through participation in their community, Kierkegaard prioritizes the inwardness of each person, which is shared only with God. This is probably the most important issue in the conflict between the two thinkers. Many philosophers would be critical of Kierkegaard's view that the individual can be considered separately from the world she inhabits. The notion of interior subjectivity may well be a secondary cultural construct, combining the influences of Christian spirituality, idealist philosophies such as those of Descartes and Kant, and Romantic ideas about the self and its creative powers. On the other hand, Kierkegaard's philosophy reflects a common experience of feeling occasionally at odds with the world and unable to express oneself fully within it. It is interesting to consider how far Kierkegaard's reaction against Hegel can be explained by his personal self-image as an outsider, and how far it is based on philosophical or religious grounds.

It is important to be aware that Kierkegaard's view of Hegelian philosophy is one amongst many possible interpretations, and the question of how far to accept this particular interpretation has to be considered when assessing Kierkegaard's objections to it. However, even if we find fault with his interpretation, the fact that Kierkegaard's critique targets rationalism, philosophy and academia in general, as well as specific aspects of Hegelian thought, means that there are further questions to consider. Is Kierkegaard seriously trying to discredit philosophy in general, and if so how successful is he? Do his criticisms of philosophy conflict with his own use of philosophical concepts and arguments? More generally, what *is* the value of intellectual reflection and academic study, and what is its relationship to questions about how best to live one's life? Where exactly do the limits of philosophical reflection lie, and how close does reason come to grasping the truth of human existence? How should philosophy approach the subject of religious faith? Kierkegaard did not invent these questions, but he asks them so insistently and with such striking originality that philosophy has taken on a new direction in order to respond to them.

CHAPTER 4

SUBJECTIVITY AND TRUTH

'Subjectivity is truth', or 'truth is subjectivity', has become a kind of
Kierkegaardian slogan, and it certainly represents an important and
influential aspect of his philosophy. This phrase appears in the
Concluding Unscientific Postscript, although the idea that truth and
subjectivity are intimately connected is present, whether explicitly
or implicitly, throughout Kierkegaard's work. The claim that
subjectivity is truth is one answer to an ancient philosophical question about the nature of truth, but it raises many further questions
– in the first place, what kind of subjectivity? and what kind of
truth? Asking these questions uncovers a complex philosophical
history of the concepts of truth and subjectivity, which Kierkegaard
draws on and responds to. From this historical perspective, the
radical and controversial character of Kierkegaard's interpretation
of truth becomes apparent. However, it is also important to have a
clear and balanced understanding of his position: to see what it
means, and what it does *not* mean. Kierkegaard's emphasis on subjectivity is not supposed to apply indiscriminately to all aspects of
knowledge, but arises from his concern to clarify what it means to
live a Christian life.

The *Concluding Unscientific Postscript* is one of Kierkegaard's
most important and widely-read works. It was published in 1846
under the pseudonym Johannes Climacus, and it is supposed to be a
'postscript' to the earlier *Philosophical Fragments*, also by Climacus.
Both of these texts are more explicitly philosophical than the other
pseudonymous works. However, the *Postscript* is also enigmatic and

contradictory: on the one hand it is a great philosophical treatise, but on the other hand it is a cruel joke, written by 'an experimental humorist' whose punch-line consists in the perverse declaration, after more than five hundred pages, that the entire book is 'superfluous'. Kierkegaard apparently intended the *Postscript* to be his last book, and perhaps its great length can be explained by the fact that he tried to fit into it everything that he had not yet written. The text includes a review of Kierkegaard's previous pseudonymous works, and also an explanation of his purpose as an author. Its main focus, however, is the question of the truth of Christianity.

Like Kierkegaard's other pseudonymous works, this text presents an alternative to the perspective of speculative – that is, Hegelian – philosophy. 'From a speculative standpoint', writes Climacus, 'Christianity is viewed as an historical phenomenon. The problem of its truth therefore becomes the problem of so interpenetrating it with thought that Christianity at last reveals itself as the eternal truth.' Climacus goes on to observe that, although speculative philosophy claims to reject all presuppositions, it assumes that Christianity is a given. His point is that everyone in Denmark is presumed to be a Christian simply by virtue of being born within a nominally Christian society – Christianity is regarded not as something to be attained, but as a matter of historical accident. Climacus imagines what would happen if a man ventured to question whether he is justified in calling himself a Christian:

> His wife would say to him: 'Dear husband of mine, how can you get such notions into your head? How can you doubt that you are a Christian? Are you not a Dane, and does not the geography say that the Lutheran form of the Christian religion is the ruling religion in Denmark? For you are surely not a Jew, nor are you a Muslim; what then can you be if not a Christian? It is a thousand years since paganism was driven out of Denmark, so I know you are not a pagan. Do you not perform your duties at the office like a conscientious civil servant; are you not a good citizen of a Christian nation, a Lutheran Christian state? So then of course you must be a Christian.'[1]

Here Climacus presents a parody of the tendency to regard Christianity in purely objective or external terms, without taking into account the individual's inward commitment, convictions and values. This man's wife does not even mention external things like going to church, reading the Bible and saying grace before meals!

The *Postscript* is divided into two books: the first, which is only about 35 pages long, discusses 'The Objective Problem Concerning the Truth of Christianity'; the second book addresses, over several hundred pages, 'The Subjective Problem; The Relation of the Subject to the Truth of Christianity; The Problem of Becoming a Christian'. The fact that the title of the book draws attention to its 'unscientific' approach is very significant, because this indicates that Kierkegaard wants to pose the question of the truth of Christianity in a new way. In his journal of 1846 he criticizes the attempt to approach spiritual matters in the same manner that a scientist would investigate the natural world:

> Scientific method becomes especially dangerous and pernicious when it would encroach also upon the sphere of the spirit. Let it deal with plants and animals and stars in that way; but to deal with the human spirit in that way is blasphemy, which only weakens ethical and religious passion . . . A dreadful sophistry spreads microscopically and telescopically into huge books, and yet in the last resort produces nothing, qualitatively understood, though it does, to be sure, cheat men out of the simple, profound and passionate wonder which gives impetus to the ethical [the attempt to live a good life] . . . *The only thing certain is the ethical-religious.*[2]

Of course, the human spirit cannot be examined under a microscope or through a telescope. But Kierkegaard is referring to theologians, philosophers and historians who try to determine the truth of Christianity from the perspective of a detached observer who is not personally involved in her subject-matter. This kind of objective, neutral approach is considered to be the model for good science (though some philosophers have questioned whether this is really possible even in the observation of natural phenomena), but Kierkegaard suggests that a scientific method cannot yield the kind of knowledge that matters most for human life. His suggestion that 'the only thing certain is the ethical-religious' is striking, because we might be inclined to assume that there is less certainty about this than about the results of scientific research. Perhaps Kierkegaard has in mind a different kind of certainty: the certainty a person feels inside when she cares deeply about something, and knows that it is right to pursue this wholeheartedly.

In *Concluding Unscientific Postscript* the pseudonym Johannes Climacus makes it clear that his view that 'subjectivity is truth' applies to what he calls 'essential knowledge'. By this he means the knowledge that is needed in order to exist. It might seem that existing is something that everyone does quite naturally, and does not require special knowledge – but Kierkegaard thinks that people often overlook the simple fact that they exist, and fail to take into account all that this involves. For human beings, it is essential to know how to be human; for an existing individual, it is essential to know how to exist; for Christians, it is essential to know how to be a Christian. Of course, every Christian is a human being, and every human being is an existing individual, and therefore living a genuinely Christian life requires knowledge about existence. 'All essential knowledge relates to existence . . . [This] knowledge has a relationship to the knower, who is essentially an existing individual . . . Only ethical and ethico-religious knowledge has an essential relationship to the existence of the knower.'[3]

One of the interesting – and also potentially confusing – features of Kierkegaard's interpretation of truth is the way it encompasses both a philosophical notion of knowledge and a theological notion of salvation. In the context of Christianity, the correspondence between truth and salvation can be summed up by Jesus's words, 'I am the way, the truth and the life', which suggest that truth and the way to salvation (or eternal life) are one and the same thing. This is the kind of truth that Kierkegaard is interested in: not just the truth that Jesus embodies, but that which is required of all those who, in following Jesus, have embarked on the task of becoming Christians and are seeking salvation. As a philosopher, Kierkegaard wants to present an accurate expression of this truth of Christianity. This is very much what Hegel had already tried to do, but Kierkegaard felt that Hegel had falsified Christianity by attempting to incorporate it into a philosophical system.

Kierkegaard highlights an opposition between the truth of Christianity and the truth of philosophy, and this means that in order to say what it means to be a Christian he creates, rather paradoxically, an anti-philosophical philosophy. To put it another way – which seems a little less paradoxical – Kierkegaard offers a philosophy of a way of life that cannot, he argues, be rationalized according to philosophical categories already in place. This new philosophy is built around ideas such as faith, inwardness, passion and subjectivity, and in trying to understand what these things mean we soon find that philosophy's traditional conception of truth has to be overturned. Kierkegaard rejects the view that the truth concerning an individual's existence is grasped in the form of an idea, as if this truth were a kind of image or representation of reality. From the point of view of the existing individual, ideas are merely possibilities that have not, at least not yet, been brought into existence. For Kierkegaard, truth does not happen when an idea accurately represents reality, but when an idea or possibility is realized, *turned into reality*, through being appropriated and acted upon by the individual. This truth is not merely thought, but lived, and this is what is needed for a religious life. Of course, salvation in the Christian tradition involves action on the part of God, but it also requires a certain kind of response from the individual, for salvation signifies a restoration of the relationship between herself and God.

This gives some indication of what Kierkegaard might mean when he suggests that the truth of Christianity must be understood in terms of subjectivity. However, the philosophical notion of subjectivity has various different senses, and it is important to clarify which of these Kierkegaard has in mind here. In general, subjectivity is opposed to objectivity, and objectivity is traditionally valued as an essential feature of the pursuit of truth. Knowledge is objective if it is unaffected by the personal interests and opinions of the knower – if it presents a transparent, unbiased and complete view of the object. Typical sources of such objective knowledge are mathematical and logical proofs, and historical facts (and these are sometimes regarded as a basis for religious faith). One way of understanding the claim that subjectivity is truth would be to argue that whatever the individual believes is true *for her*, regardless of what is objectively the case. On this view, truth is completely relative, and it does not even make sense to say that someone is mistaken about the truth. This is certainly not what Kierkegaard is suggesting, and this means that we have to consider a different notion of subjectivity.

In philosophy, the term 'subject' refers to a generalized, universal notion of the individual: philosophers might talk about the thinking subject, the knowing subject, the moral subject, and so on. (Most philosophers have argued that the human subject is distinguished by its capacity for rational thought, which in turn makes it capable of moral action. Kierkegaard, however, claims that the essence of the human subject is not reason, but passion.) 'Subjectivity is truth' means that truth is *a way of being a subject*, or a way of existing as a human being. Kierkegaard says that subjective truth is a matter of *how* – how one lives – whereas objective truth is a matter of *what* one knows or believes:

> Objectively the emphasis is on **what** is said; subjectively the emphasis is on **how** it is said . . . But this is not to be understood as manner, modulation of voice, oral delivery, etc., but it is to be understood as the relation of the existing person, in his very existence, to what is said. Objectively, the question is only about categories of thought; subjectively, about inwardness . . . Only in subjectivity is there decision, whereas wanting to become objective is untruth. The passion of the infinite, not its content, is the deciding factor, for its content is precisely itself. In this way the subjective 'how' and subjectivity are the truth.[4]

In the context of Christianity, an example of objective truth (or untruth) would be the doctrine of Jesus's resurrection. If we interpret the claim that 'subjectivity is truth' as meaning that whatever I think or believe is true for me, we are making the mistake of focusing on 'what' rather than 'how'. Kierkegaard prioritizes the individual's private relationship to God, and his favourite categories of faith, commitment, passion and inwardness signify the way in which this relationship should be lived if it is truly religious, truly Christian.

In emphasizing subjectivity rather than objectivity, or 'how' rather than 'what', Kierkegaard is claiming that truth is not merely an epistemological issue (that is, a matter of knowledge), but an ethical issue. Kierkegaard uses the term 'ethical' in different ways, but in this case it means being concerned about one's existence and raising the question of how best to live. Unlike most philosophers, Kierkegaard is critical of the role of knowledge in this kind of ethical enquiry. He argues that it is possible to engage in intellectual reflection for its own sake – perhaps to comfort or distract oneself; perhaps to satisfy a desire to be clever, and to gain recognition from other people – without bringing this to bear on one's own life. The existing individual can, quite literally, become lost in thought: Kierkegaard points out that it is contradictory to claim that the purpose of human life is abstract knowledge, since abstraction means a movement *away from* existence.

In *Concluding Unscientific Postscript* the pseudonym Johannes Climacus suggests that objective knowledge alone cannot help a person to live her life well. He concedes that objectivity seems to promise a certain security, and that any subjectivity which refused to take account of objective truth would be in danger of slipping into madness. But he points out that 'the absence of inwardness [is] also madness'. Climacus invites us to imagine a patient who, having just escaped from a mental hospital, is worried that he will be recognized and taken back there. This deluded man thinks to himself:

> 'What you need to do, then, is to convince everyone completely, by the objective truth of what you say, that all is well as far as your sanity is concerned.' As he is walking along and pondering this, he sees a skittle ball lying on the ground. He picks it up and puts it in the tail of his coat. At every step he takes, this ball bumps him, if you please, on his bottom, and every time it bumps him he says, 'Boom! The earth is round!' He arrives in the capital city and immediately visits one of his friends. He want to convince him that he is not crazy and therefore walks back and forth, saying continually 'Boom! The earth is round!'[5]

In attempting to prove his sanity, the patient draws attention to his madness and gives himself away. In this case, stating 'a generally accepted and generally respected universal truth' provides no security, because the man lacks the ability to judge the appropriateness of his behaviour. He is unable to reflect on himself. For Kierkegaard, this madman can be compared to a philosopher who does nothing but proclaim the results of logical calculations, when he is supposed to be in the business of seeking wisdom, which must begin with an awareness of his own existence. For both the escaped lunatic and the philosopher, it is not the content of the truth that is wrong, but the context and the way in which it is asserted: 'it was clear to the doctor that the patient was not yet cured; though it is not to be thought that the cure would consist in getting him to accept the opinion that the earth is flat'. Of course, an objective falsehood is no better than an objective truth – in fact, this would be even worse – for the problem is with objectivity itself. Kierkegaard is suggesting that the philosopher who tries to show that he is wise by proclaiming objective truth is as absurd as the madman who tries to prove his sanity in the same way.

As I have suggested, 'subjectivity is truth' has both philosophical and theological significance. On the one hand this understanding of truth is opposed to Hegelian philosophy, and on the other hand it is opposed to the idea of Christendom. Even though Hegel is in fact very much concerned with both the 'what' and 'how' senses of truth, Kierkegaard focuses on Hegel's claim that reason's task is to grasp the nature of reality, as it is objectively, and that truth finds its highest expression in philosophical, conceptual knowledge. Kierkegaard's criticism of objectivity challenges the view, apparently held by Hegelians such as Martensen, that the truth of Christianity is to be found in a particular interpretation of theological doctrine. He also regards reliance on an objective understanding of truth as symptomatic of the spiritual malaise and hypocrisy that he finds in Christendom, where, he argues, Christianity has become merely a matter of *what* people claim to believe, and *what* they are seen to be doing. For Kierkegaard, there is a link between Hegelian philosophy and Christendom, because in both cases being a Christian means participating in a certain form of social life – and this, he argues, allows people to neglect the inward spiritual life that matters most of all.

This does not necessarily mean that what people believe and what they do is irrelevant. Kierkegaard does not say that believing in Jesus's resurrection or going to church on Sundays is unimportant – rather, he is pointing out that these sorts of things are not the whole of the Christian life. Assuming that an individual *does* believe in the resurrection and *does* attend church regularly, there is a further question about *how* she does these things, and for Kierkegaard this question is of the utmost significance. People can go through the motions of attending church services and professing their Christian beliefs without passion, and without examining themselves honestly and asking whether they are really wholehearted in their faith. In fact, it is possible to use the 'objective' aspects of Christianity as a way to avoid raising this question. A willingness to question the authenticity of one's own spiritual life, and to keep questioning it continually, is a first and essential step towards becoming a Christian *subjectively*, and therefore truthfully.

But how are we to define truth in this context? Clearly, it is not a matter of demonstrating the validity of a logical argument, or of proving the accuracy of an historical fact. In the *Concluding Unscientific Postscript* Johannes Climacus points out that philosophers usually understand truth in terms of a correspondence between thought and being, between reflection and reality. Empiricist philosophers (those who treat experience as the source of knowledge) define truth as the conformity of thinking with being, whereas idealist philosophers (those who place the intellect before experience) define it as the conformity of being with thinking. Both, however, have a static model of truth that is based on a relationship of agreement between thinking and existence.

Kierkegaard offers a different interpretation of truth, which draws on the notions of authenticity, fidelity and honesty. Authenticity, or genuineness, is a correspondence not between an idea and an object, but between a person's inwardness and her actions. We feel that we are inauthentic if we behave in a way that is not a true expression of our inner conviction, and because most of us are familiar with this experience it is often quite easy to identify this kind of artificiality in other people. Fidelity means being true to someone, something, or even oneself (and in this case it is similar to authenticity) over a period of time. Honesty is not just a matter of telling the truth, but of being willing to reflect on oneself and bring to light things one prefers to keep concealed. These kinds of truth are distinct, but closely connected: not only are they all ways of being a subject, they are also ways of relating to other subjects. From the point of view of the existing individual, this account of truth is essential to the task of becoming a Christian – for Christianity, as well as being 'objectively' a theological doctrine and an historical, social phenomenon, is a particular way of being a subject *in relationship to* God, and to other individuals.

Subjective truth is an ethical quality, and it has validity only when it is brought into existence; as long as it is a mere idea, or a mere possibility, it has no value. It is little use to think about being authentic, faithful or honest if one's actions turn out to be inauthentic, disloyal or deceitful. Kierkegaard is interested in a kind of truth that happens only when it is actualized. Here, truth is not the result of a correspondence or a conformity between thinking and being; rather, it is produced by a *transition* from thinking to being. Ideas or possibilities are brought into existence, made real, by being acted upon. In the sphere of subjectivity, truth that is not lived is no truth at all.

Authenticity, fidelity and honesty are ways of being: 'how' rather than 'what'. It is more accurate, however, to describe them as ways of *becoming*, for Kierkegaard emphasizes that existence is always a process of becoming. Truth as subjectivity is not fixed or eternal, for life is continually changing. On this point Kierkegaard is influenced by Hegel's attempt to reinterpret truth in accordance with the dynamic quality of existence itself, but of course his insistence on the perspective of the existing individual leads him in a direction that is quite opposed to Hegel's logic of mediation. Both Hegel and Kierkegaard recognize that existence is characterized by becoming, movement and change, but whereas Hegel asks how one can know the truth under these conditions, Kierkegaard asks how one can *be* true under these conditions.

In *Repetition*, and again in *Stages on Life's Way*, Kierkegaard uses the story of a broken engagement to illustrate this problem. A young man has asked his girlfriend to marry him, but now he finds himself wanting to end the engagement. Because he has changed his mind – and he cannot really be blamed for this, since his original intention to marry the girl was sincere – there is a conflict between being true (faithful) to his fiancée, and being true (authentic and honest) about his new feelings. Whether he breaks off the engagement or gets married, he seems to be guilty of untruth. This situation – which clearly reflects Kierkegaard's own experience with Regine – shows that truth itself changes when there is a change in the individual's inwardness: being authentic might involve different things at different times. This means that the kind of truthfulness that is expressed through authenticity, fidelity and honesty must be repeatedly renewed if it is to remain constant, for none of these qualities can be achieved once and for all.

The example of the broken engagement also highlights the fact that subjective truth cannot be based on knowledge: the fiancé *did not know* that he was going to change his mind. (If he had known, then it was not a genuine change, and the engagement was inauthentic from the start.) Because the movement of existence is oriented towards the future, it involves an encounter with the unknown. This means that subjectivity is always open, able to grow and to take on new shapes and determinations – and the same must be said of truth also. Becoming a Christian, or becoming any other kind of subject, is an open-ended task that stretches through the individual's whole lifetime. Truth is not an object that can be possessed, but a transient quality that slips away as soon as it is actualized, and so needs to be brought into being again and again.

For this reason the concept of repetition is the key to Kierkegaard's account of subjective truth. In *Repetition* the pseudonym Constantin

Constantius sets up a theoretical framework for making sense of the young fiancé's broken engagement: he suggests that repetition should replace the notion of recollection, which is the basis for Plato's doctrine of knowledge. Recollection and repetition are both processes through which truth is reached, but they move in opposite directions: recollection finds a truth that already exists, but has been forgotten, whereas through repetition the individual renews or recreates the truth *relating to her subjectivity*, bringing it into existence once again. In other words, recollection is oriented towards the past, whereas repetition is oriented towards the future. Recollection seeks the truth as *knowledge*, but repetition produces the kind of truth that belongs to *life*: 'When the Greeks said that *all knowledge is recollection* they affirmed that all that is has been; when one says that *life is a repetition* one affirms that existence which has been now becomes'.[6] Repetition can produce a continuous, stable identity: although subjectivity is always becoming new, it can repeatedly commit itself to its previous values, and thus unify its past, present and future. Through repetition the individual is able to be true both to herself and to others; betrayal, infidelity and broken promises are due to a failure of repetition.

If subjective truth is to be more than momentary, it has to be repeated continually. Whereas traditional objective truth – the truth as knowledge – is threatened by the change that characterizes existence, Kierkegaard's interpretation of truth is actually based on the movement of becoming. The constancy of fidelity is not static, but a result of repetition. Closely connected to repetition is the idea of passion. To some extent, the two concepts are interchangeable for Kierkegaard: *Repetition* is one of his earliest books, and although he here presents repetition as an important new philosophical concept he hardly mentions it in subsequent texts; but passion plays a similar role to repetition. (Perhaps Kierkegaard prefers to talk of passion because it is less abstract, more human, than repetition.) Passion, like repetition, signifies a kind of spiritual energy that gives continuity and stability to the individual's existence. When one is passionate about something, one returns to it again and again; passion provides focus, momentum and direction. Passion is a much fuller concept than repetition: it implies valuing something and being concerned about it; it also suggests love and suffering, which are important themes within Christianity, and therefore within Kierkegaard's philosophy too. In fact, Kierkegaard suggests that passion is the most essential aspect of

human nature, and this means that being passionate is a measure of being truly human.

In the context of Christian faith, passion is needed because, Kierkegaard argues, the object of faith – the doctrine of the incarnation and resurrection – is objectively uncertain. It is not difficult to challenge the historical accuracy of the gospels, and it is impossible to prove through rational argument that Jesus was actually God living a human life, and that he rose from his tomb after being dead for three days. In fact, Kierkegaard suggests that the idea of a being who is at once human and divine is self-contradictory, and therefore logically unacceptable. In both *Philosophical Fragments* and *Concluding Unscientific Postscript* Johannes Climacus argues that Christianity is profoundly paradoxical, 'an absurdity to the understanding':

> Christianity has declared itself to be the eternal essential truth which has come into being in time. It has proclaimed itself as the *Paradox*, and it has required of the individual the inwardness of faith . . . It is impossible more strongly to express the fact that subjectivity is truth . . . Suppose Christianity never intended to be understood; suppose that, in order to express this, and to prevent anyone from misguidedly entering upon the objective way, it has declared itself to be the paradox. Suppose it wished to have significance only for existing individuals, and essentially for existing individuals in inwardness, in the inwardness of faith; which cannot be expressed more definitely than in the proposition that Christianity is the absurd, held fast in the passion of the infinite . . . Suppose Christianity is not a matter of knowledge, so that increased knowledge is of no avail, except to make it easier to fall into the confusion of considering Christianity as a matter of knowledge.[7]

The objective uncertainty of Christianity is, according to Kierkegaard, a positive thing from a spiritual point of view, because it requires the individual to believe actively and passionately – to put her energy into faith, and to keep this going in the face of everything that might undermine it. Certainty has to come from the side of subjectivity – where it takes the form of passion, commitment and faith – since it cannot be found within Christian doctrine itself. This means that faith must be an expression of a person's freedom,

whereas if something is objectively and evidently true, one is simply compelled to believe it.

THE AESTHETIC, THE ETHICAL AND THE RELIGIOUS

There are as many ways of being a subject as there are existing individuals, for no two subjectivities are exactly alike. However, Kierkegaard distinguishes between three main types of subjectivity: aesthetic, ethical and religious. These categories, which are often described as 'stages' or 'spheres' of existence, are introduced in his very first book, *Either/Or*, and they appear throughout the pseudonymous authorship. There has been a lot of debate amongst Kierkegaard's readers about how to understand them: do they refer to different types of people, or to different phases in one person's life? Is it best to think of them as stages or as spheres of existence? How are the different categories related to one another? We will return to these questions once we have looked at the aesthetic, ethical and religious types of subjectivity in some detail. But to begin with, it is worth asking about the purpose of these categories: why does Kierkegaard make these particular distinctions? In general, philosophers make distinctions in order to clarify something – so what is Kierkegaard trying to clarify?

Aesthetic, ethical and religious are different types of subjectivity, and therefore they refer to 'how' one lives, rather than 'what' one believes or does. In *Concluding Unscientific Postscript*, Johannes Climacus suggests that 'when the different spheres [of existence] are not decisively distinguished from one another, confusion reigns everywhere'. He gives the example of being interested in another person's existence. In the sphere of intellectual reflection (which, as we shall see, is itself part of the aesthetic sphere), 'the maximum attainment is to become altogether indifferent to the thinker's reality'. Here Climacus is arguing that being interested in the life of, say, a philosopher or a scientist will only get in the way of understanding her theories. However, in the sphere of faith (that is, the religious sphere), interest in the teacher's existence is essential: 'the object of faith is the reality of another, and the relationship is one of infinite interest'. Although there may be a superficial resemblance between a religious person and someone who misguidedly takes an interest in the existence of a thinker, these two are, in fact, worlds apart. Climacus uses the distinctions between different spheres of existence to insist that it is inappropriate to approach Christianity from an intellectual perspective:

> Christianity is no doctrine concerning the unity of the divine and the human, or concerning the identity of the subject and the object; nor is it any other of the logical transcriptions of Christianity. If Christianity were a doctrine, the relationship to it would not be one of faith, for only an intellectual type of relationship can correspond to a doctrine. Christianity is therefore not a doctrine, but the fact that God has existed . . . Faith constitutes a sphere all by itself, and every misunderstanding of Christianity may be at once recognised by its transforming it into a doctrine, transferring it to the sphere of the intellectual. The maximum of attainment within the sphere of the intellectual, namely, to realise an entire indifference as to the reality of the teacher, is in the sphere of faith at the opposite end of the scale. The maximum of attainment within the sphere of faith is to become infinitely interested in the reality of the teacher.[8]

This passage makes it clear that one function of the spheres of existence is to resist a rationalist – and especially an Hegelian – interpretation of Christianity. More generally, the claim that 'faith constitutes a sphere all by itself' is intended to prevent the religious life being reduced to a merely intellectual adherence to a doctrine, or to obedience to an ethical code.

As we saw in Chapter 2, Kierkegaard's texts address the reader personally, as an existing individual, and encourage her to reflect on her own existence. The categories of aesthetic, ethical and religious are an aid to this kind of reflection: they help the reader to realize the truth about herself, to see herself more clearly. Kierkegaard has great insight into the complexity of human nature, and especially into the tendency to deceive oneself about who one really is. Focusing on objective things is a very good way to avoid the truth about one's subjectivity. To use a previous example: someone goes through the motions of Christianity without being inwardly authentic; she might *think* she is being religious, but when she considers herself in relation to Kierkegaard's existential categories she will recognize that she has more in common with the aesthetic personality. The categories are there to instruct people who believe that they already know what it means to be ethical or religious. In particular, they show sophisticated, educated readers that being knowledgeable or intelligent does not mean that there is no progress to be made – existentially speaking – for even an eminent theologian or an accomplished professor of philosophy might live completely within the aesthetic sphere.

The spheres of existence represent different possible ways of life that are available to each individual. It is important to note that all of these possibilities are distinctively human: for Kierkegaard, it is the fact that we have possibilities *at all* that marks us out from other creatures. A plant or an animal could not be regarded as aesthetic, ethical or religious: these are types of *existence*, and Kierkegaard uses this term 'existence' to refer to ways of being that reach beyond the biological conditions of life, such as the need for food and shelter, and the drive to reproduce and to avoid danger. In this sense, to exist means to take up a stance *in relation* to one's life and world, rather than merely functioning instinctively as an organism.

The aesthetic mode of existence is characterized by the pursuit of personal satisfaction. The aesthete lives for the pleasures of the moment, and tends to have a refined sensitivity to beauty. Some people might seek pleasure in contemplating the physical beauty of other people, works of art, or the natural world, whereas others prefer the intellectual pleasure that comes from reflecting on ideas. The aesthetic individual has a rich imaginative life, and seeks novelty as a means to stimulate her imagination. She values spontaneity, creativity and freedom, and she avoids commitment and rejects social conventions as these would impose restrictions on her life – most of all, she wants to live *poetically*. Like a novelist, an actor, or an artist, the aesthete plays and experiments with different possibilities. An interest in fashionable clothes, literature, places and attitudes is a typical aesthetic trait. Kierkegaard's portrayal of the aesthetic sphere is clearly shaped by the intellectual and cultural phenomenon of Romanticism, which was extremely influential in nineteenth-century Europe.

The aesthetic sphere is not confined to artists, intellectuals and beautiful people. The seducer is a typical aesthetic figure, and a seducer's diary is included in Part I of *Either/Or*. This character spends his time chasing different women – different possibilities, different ideals – and derives his satisfaction from the intoxicating phase of first love. However, he is not willing to open up his imaginative inner world to the reality of another person, and none of his romances are actually consummated. He is not prepared to limit his possible enjoyment of every woman by entering into a relationship with any particular woman. The seducer does not love women for who they really are, but creates ideal versions of them in his imagination; he needs constantly to vary the object of his affections in order to sustain the novelty that his pleasure requires.

Kierkegaard's attitude towards the aesthetic sphere is ambivalent, but usually it is quite negative. The aesthete in *Either/Or* suffers from boredom, melancholy and a sense of emptiness; his writings show that his way of life is ultimately nihilistic, and tends to lead to despair since pleasure is so transient. (Does an aesthetic existence *produce* nihilism, because it values nothing but pleasure, which is always fleeting? Or is it a *consequence* of nihilism, since the person who finds that nothing is valuable in itself concludes that she may as well devote her life to seeking pleasure?) Although the aesthetic form of subjectivity is self-interested, it is actually based on a very weak sense of self, since all action is motivated by momentary moods, desires and inclinations. None of these can provide a person with a stable identity. And although the aesthete refuses to accept limitations, she actually lacks freedom – for Kierkegaard defines freedom as a person's power or capacity to act, to become something, and to give direction to her life.

The qualities that belong to the aesthetic sphere are extremely valuable for writing poetry or fiction, for appreciating works of art, and for evaluating philosophical systems. However, as a way of existing Kierkegaard finds it deficient. An important feature of the aesthetic form of life is the failure to engage properly with the reality of one's own existence, or with the reality of another person's subjectivity. The aesthete remains in the sphere of ideas and possibilities, and is unable to turn these into something real. (Of course, it is not easy to say what is meant by reality in the context of subjectivity; in *Concluding Unscientific Postscript* Johannes Climacus defines reality in terms of 'inwardness', but this is similarly difficult to grasp concretely.) Kierkegaard is not suggesting that everyone who enjoys beautiful things or exciting ideas is confined to the aesthetic sphere; rather, an aesthete is someone who thinks that pleasure is the *only* value, the *only* thing worth living for. In fact, the positive aspects of the aesthetic life can continue to have a role within the ethical and religious spheres.

The ethical individual is more or less the exact opposite of the aesthete. In general, being ethical means attempting to act in a morally correct way. This tends to be understood in terms of conformity to a law, whether this takes the form of an inner sense of right and wrong, a moral code taught by a religious tradition, legislation enforced by the state, or simply the customs and conventions followed by a particular community. Ethical action is usually worked out in terms of a vocabulary of rights and duties. From a philosophical point of view there are, of course, many different accounts of ethics – for example, Aristotle's ethics focuses on cultivating virtues; John Stuart Mill's utilitarian ethics is based on the principle of maximizing happiness; Kant's ethics stresses moral autonomy and respect for others – but all of these urge the individual to rise above her immediate, self-serving desires for the sake of the community as a whole.

For Kierkegaard, the ethical sphere certainly includes this concern for moral action. However, it also has a more 'existential' dimension: becoming ethical means taking responsibility for one's own life, making choices and commitments, and recognizing the significance of freedom and action. In short, the ethical person takes herself and her life seriously. By exercising her freedom she gives shape to her inner life; by sustaining her commitments (through repeatedly renewing them) she gives this inwardness continuity and stability through time. Unlike the aesthete, the ethical individual accepts the limitations that come with having a family and a job, respecting social conventions and participating in a community. Taking on these roles provides a strong personal identity, and offers a certain security, stability and self-assurance. Although being ethical involves a concern for others, it also consolidates a sense of self.

Like the aesthetic mode of existence, the ethical sphere has limitations. In fact, Kierkegaard claims that it too will lead to despair. The ethical person strives for a moral perfection that is unattainable, and must continually battle against bad habits and selfish inclinations. Through repetition she might achieve a relatively enduring self-identity, but actually this is fragile and at every moment vulnerable to forces beyond her control. The world that gives meaning to the individual's existence can change in an instant. The solidity and security of the ethical sphere is, in fact, an illusion. Although Kierkegaard recognizes the value of the ethical life, from a religious perspective he regards it as a misguided assertion of human self-sufficiency. Because ethical judgements are always subject to human error, there is no final certainty to be found within the ethical sphere;

this can lead to profound self-doubt, or to a mistaken sense of self-righteousness – and both are spiritually paralysing.

The religious individual bases her existence upon her relationship to God. Whilst the ethical sphere focuses on finite, worldly concerns, and accepts the limitations that these bring, the religious type of subjectivity opens up to an eternal dimension that includes both God's presence and the prospect of eternal life. These are encountered subjectively, in faith and with passion, rather than as objective facts. Faith involves understanding that one is not self-sufficient, but dependent on God's grace. This is inseparable from a consciousness of sin: whereas the ethical person strives for moral goodness, the starting-point of the religious life is a recognition that one is a sinner. This does not mean that the religious individual abandons the ideal of righteousness, but she is aware that this cannot be achieved through her own efforts, and that she is in need of forgiveness.

In the *Postscript* Climacus distinguishes between two types of religiousness, which he calls 'A' and 'B' – although it is quite clear that 'B' refers to Christianity, whereas 'A' is supposed to incorporate all other religions. In Religion A, the eternal or the divine is regarded as a quality within each individual, which needs to be attended to, cultivated, and brought more to the centre of her life. Kierkegaard thinks that all pre-Christian religions, including the authentic philosophical life taught by Socrates, are immanent in this way: they present a spiritual path that is essentially a human quest for the divine. This type of religiousness tends to involve surrendering one's attachments to finite things and ceasing to hope for satisfaction in worldly terms, in exchange for a relationship to God. Religion A offers comfort, security and peace to the soul, but from a Christian perspective it does not place enough emphasis on human sinfulness and the need for salvation.

Religion B, or Christianity, teaches that only God's love and grace, manifested in His incarnation in Jesus Christ, can offer salvation. This religion emphasizes the gravity of sin, and therefore regards the unity of the divine and human natures as paradoxical, rather than as a natural, original state that merely has to be uncovered. Kierkegaard describes sin as a state of 'untruth': the Christian can acknowledge her sinfulness by turning around the claim that subjectivity is truth, and asserting instead that 'subjectivity is untruth'. This highlights the way in which Kierkegaard's interpretation of truth incorporates the religious notion of salvation. Because sin marks a radical difference between man and God, reconciliation can only be brought about by God. Christianity teaches that this reconciliation has actually happened through the earthly life and death of Jesus – and this, for Kierkegaard, is a paradox that exceeds our scope for understanding.

Furthermore, Christian faith itself is paradoxical because the individual bases her eternal happiness (that is, her hope for eternal life in heaven) upon the historical event of the incarnation. Whilst in Religion A the individual sacrifices her temporal interests for the sake of the eternal, in Religion B eternity and temporality are held together simultaneously, although the contradiction between them is maintained. The Christian does renounce her worldly concerns, but she also continues to hope for happiness within her life. Kierkegaard admits that this attitude is contradictory, and therefore absurd – but hoping in this way is, he argues, an expression of faith and passion. Through this faith a person remains receptive to God's grace, and will regard whatever befalls her as a gift from Him: what comes as a genuine gift has to be unexpected, and yet a certain expectation is required in order to be ready and open enough to receive it. In the *Postscript* Climacus suggests that many of his contemporaries who call themselves Christians do not actually reach beyond the immanent spirituality of Religion A.

In addition to the aesthetic, ethical and religious spheres of existence, Kierkegaard identifies 'boundary zones', or transitional phases, between them. He suggests that irony is the boundary that separates the aesthetic from the ethical, although it is probably more accurate to say that irony is still within the aesthetic, but points beyond itself to ethics. This idea that irony lies between the two spheres is rather perplexing – not least because irony is itself a rather slippery concept. It is difficult to offer a clear definition of irony since it is used in different, though related, senses. It is often confused with the narrower and more straightforward concept of sarcasm, which means saying one thing while meaning the opposite. Irony also involves a doubleness of meaning, but this is not limited to linguistic meaning: situations as well as statements can be ironic. Irony generally arises from a disjunction, or a contradiction – between what is intended and what is actually the case; between an apparent meaning and what is actually intended; or between the purpose of an action and what results from it. Irony is the sort of thing that may or may not be detected; it has a certain cryptic, covert quality, and creates a distance between people who are in the know and those who are unaware of the deeper meaning.

One example of irony, which fascinates Kierkegaard, is that practised by Socrates: his questions are often ironic, because they pretend to seek wisdom from the interlocutor, whilst actually highlighting his ignorance; furthermore, by making the interlocutor's ignorance apparent, Socrates leads him to greater wisdom. In other words, Socrates' questions *do* seek to extract wisdom, but indirectly, and not in the way that he makes explicit. This is a good example of irony, as it highlights the contrast with sarcasm: whereas a sarcastic comment fairly transparently means the exact opposite, an ironic statement may in fact mean what it says, but not in the sense that seems most obvious. Another well-known example of irony appears in the Gospel of John, chapter 18, where the high priest Caiaphas suggests that it is 'expedient that one man should die for the people'. Caiaphas means that executing a controversial character such as Jesus will help to restore order and ease tensions between the Romans and the Jews. He is not being deliberately ironic, but Christians (like, no doubt, the author of John's Gospel) will find irony in his words because they see a deeper, theological meaning – that Jesus's death atones for the sins of humanity.

How, then, are we to understand Kierkegaard's claim that irony is the boundary between the aesthetic and ethical spheres? I do not pretend to have a conclusive answer to this question, but I will offer some suggestions. In the *Postscript*, where the idea of 'boundary zones' is put forward, Climacus suggests that irony expresses the contradiction 'between the internal and the external'. There is certainly irony in the aesthetic way of life insofar as the individual's intentions lead to quite opposite results: the aesthete seeks pleasure, yet ends up in despair; she craves excitement and novelty, but becomes bored even with these; she is self-interested, and yet she lacks a clear sense of self. Usually, however, the aesthete is absorbed in her inner world of fleeting ideas, fantasies, moods and sensations, and is unable to reflect on her existence as a whole. Grasping irony requires taking a step back from immediate experience and finding a standpoint outside the situation from which to perceive the disparity between ideality and reality. In this way, the aesthete can come to see herself more clearly. Of course, this ironic standpoint is just another possibility, and therefore it is not yet beyond the aesthetic sphere: a separate, existential movement must be made to actualize this possibility. But at least the aesthete can, through irony, grasp the distinction between possibility and actuality – and this brings her closer to the point of really engaging with the reality of her existence. Irony has a self-undermining quality, and this helps the aesthete to understand that her way of life is untenable.

Kierkegaard suggests that the 'boundary zone' between the ethical and religious spheres is humour. Whilst moving from the aesthetic to the ethical involves taking oneself *more* seriously, moving from the ethical to the religious involves taking oneself *less* seriously. The ethical individual – perhaps when she is close to despair – might suddenly see the funny side of her absurd struggle to live a completely upright life. She is striving with utmost determination for something that is impossible to attain! She might even laugh at her own seriousness, which is, in the bigger scheme of things, quite ridiculous. Humour arises from the insight that human existence is at once unbearably heavy and ultra-light; full of significance, and yet pretty insignificant; overwhelmingly difficult and very, very easy. Humour is transitional because, like irony, it brings a complete shift in perspective, and helps people to see themselves differently.

KIERKEGAARD'S SPHERES OF EXISTENCE

Kierkegaard's description of the aesthetic, ethical and religious spheres of existence outlines fundamentally different kinds of subjectivity. What, then, is the connection between his account of the spheres and his claim that 'subjectivity is truth'? Is one sphere supposed to be more truthful, more authentic, than another? A few commentators on Kierkegaard's authorship have argued that there is no hierarchy amongst the spheres – and it is certainly fair to say that each sphere has its own kind of truth. On the whole, though, it seems clear that there is a progression from the aesthetic to the ethical to the religious, and that Kierkegaard values the Christian way of life more highly than the others. After all, this is what his whole authorship is directed towards, or, rather *how* it was directed.

When we examined Kierkegaard's view that 'subjectivity is truth', we saw that this interpretation of truth emphasizes fidelity, authenticity and honesty. These qualities, or ways of being a subject, are sustained through the movement of becoming that is essential to existence. Kierkegaard suggests that truth happens in the individual's inwardness: it involves passion, or repetition, and expresses a kind of potency, power or capacity that is synonymous with human freedom. According to these criteria for truth, it seems that the movement from the aesthetic to the religious is a progression from a less to a more truthful form of life. The spheres become increasingly inward, increasingly passionate, and increasingly powerful.

The aesthetic personality does have an inner life, but this is like a screen across which ideas, images and possibilities pass, without shaping the self in any way. For Kierkegaard, inwardness means a sort of spiritual depth, and this is what the aesthete lacks. She is indifferent to the fact that she, or anyone else, actually exists; in a spiritual sense she is impotent, absorbed in reflection and unable to make the choices and commitments that would make her life more meaningful. The ethical individual, by contrast, deepens her inwardness by taking responsibility for her life; she has a sincere concern for herself and others; she is capable of acting purposefully, and of becoming a particular kind of self. The religious person surrenders to God the strong sense of self that is built up in the ethical sphere. She opens herself fully, empties herself out, to something beyond herself – to God's transcendent power. Her relationship to God puts worldly concerns in a different perspective, and inwardness becomes, in a sense, the only thing that matters. This does not mean that life is not lived fully. The religious form of life is the most passionate human possibility: Kierkegaard says that Christian faith, because it cannot be based on reason, requires unlimited passion in order to be sustained.

I have described the spheres of existence as different possibilities. Kierkegaard is very alert to the fact that human life, uniquely, includes the dimension of possibility: we are aware not only of what is, but of what could be. In fact, each sphere of existence involves a different relationship to possibility – we might say that each sphere is a possible way of responding to the human dimension of possibility. The aesthete is entranced by possibilities: she contemplates and explores them, plays and experiments with them. Because she does not grasp the meaning of her freedom, she wants her possibilities to be infinite, unlimited. In choosing and committing to one possibility, we always exclude others, and therefore the aesthete is unwilling to make the decisions that, ironically, would realize the freedom she thinks she is pursuing. Everything is possible, but nothing happens. In the ethical sphere the emphasis is on actualizing possibilities, and thus exercising freedom. An ethical person accepts the finitude and constraints that this brings, and these limitations produce a clearer, stronger, more fully-formed self. In the religious sphere the finite and the infinite are brought and held together: there is a profound acceptance of the self's limitations, but nevertheless the religious person continues to believe in infinite possibilities. Kierkegaard once suggested that God is: 'that all things are possible'. The Christian, in fact, believes the impossible: that a paradoxical incarnation of God has existed in time, and that this historical event has the power to bestow eternal salvation. She believes that the impossible will become actual – through God's power, or grace (it cannot be through her own power, otherwise it would not in fact be impossible). When she decides to become a Christian, the individual actualizes a possibility in the ethical sense, but this commitment *means* being fully open and receptive to God, and thus letting go the merely-human boundaries of the self.

Of course, all of the spheres of existence – and the characters and scenarios that exemplify them – are possibilities that are presented in Kierkegaard's texts. He was aware that his own activity as an author was, in a way, aesthetic, and could certainly be regarded in purely aesthetic terms. Perhaps the reason why Kierkegaard published his religious discourses *on the same day* as the pseudonymous books is to show that these 'aesthetic' works have an intention that takes them beyond the aesthetic sphere. They include the irony that points towards the ethical form of life – a pseudo-Socratic irony that seeks to elicit an existential response. In a sense Kierkegaard's authorship is at once aesthetic, ethical *and* religious: the pseudonymous texts assume the appearance of the aesthetic sphere, exploring the different possibilities available to human subjectivity, but they also try to encourage the reader's ethical awakening by highlighting the importance of becoming a self through choices and commitments. This process, argues Kierkegaard, is essential to the religious task of 'becoming a Christian'. He attempts to perform, as an author, a kind of therapeutic action that seeks to improve the spiritual health of the reader. This action itself belongs to the ethical sphere: in becoming an author, Kierkegaard chooses and commits to (through his long days at his writing desk) a way of life, to the exclusion of other possibilities – marrying Regine, becoming a country parson, becoming a university professor. He finds a role, a vocation, that makes his life meaningful, and in this role he pursues his concern for the subjectivity of others. No doubt Kierkegaard was aware of the ironic and humorous aspects of his situation: he expresses this continually in his writing.

This view of Kierkegaard's life and works gives some indication of the way the spheres of existence can include one another. The perspective and the resources of the aesthetic sphere can be put to use within one's ethical life; the self created in the ethical sphere is what the religious person must surrender and open up to God. This means that moving from one sphere to another does not mean leaving the lower one behind altogether. In a sense the theory of successive stages of existence represents not a progression, but a deepening: the development of a more profound inwardness. This is perhaps why Kierkegaard switched from 'stages' to 'spheres' in his discussions of the aesthetic, ethical and religious forms of life. However, the deepening process must take place over time, and so it is not necessarily wrong to think of a linear progression through the spheres. Even if we think of this as an inward movement, we also need to remember that Kierkegaard claims that the transition between the spheres can only be accomplished by a leap. This is because the spheres are qualitatively different from one another. There is nothing within the aesthetic sphere that enables the individual to actualize a possibility, or make a decision: as soon as this happens, she has already moved on to the ethical sphere. And within the ethical sphere – that is, in merely human terms – there is no means to relate to God: as soon as this happens, the individual has become religious. This highlights the difference between Kierkegaard's and Hegel's accounts of becoming: where Hegel emphasizes mediation, Kierkegaard insists on a leap.

A big question that remains is whether or not we agree with Kierkegaard's account of the aesthetic, ethical and religious spheres of existence. Do we accept the values that this interpretation of subjectivity puts forward? In a sense, the whole thing is supposed to clarify what it means to be a Christian, and if we do not share Kierkegaard's religious perspective then we may want to question his view that the aesthetic and ethical forms of life are, as human possibilities, deficient in some way. Nietzsche, for example, rejects belief in God and other Christian values, and argues that without these we are left to make up our own values – and the only criteria available to us are those of the aesthetic sphere. Whereas Kierkegaard describes the aesthetic way of life as spiritually weak, Nietzsche admires its creativity, spontaneity and autonomy; indeed, he regards these qualities as God-like, and the very highest expression of human power. From a less exalted point of view, those who live ethically might challenge the claim that there is something lacking from the life of a person who, with no thought of God and no need of salvation, puts her love and energy into her family and friends; works conscientiously in a worthwhile job; tries to be honest and kind to others; gives what she can to those in need; and is inwardly committed to all these things.

The distinctions that Kierkegaard makes within the religious sphere itself are even more questionable. Is revering nature, or being moved by the beauty of a fleeting moment, or gaining insight through meditation, or simply worshipping God, really inferior to having a relationship to Christ? Why should we accept Kierkegaard's spiritual hierarchy, when he has a simplistic grasp of other traditions and knows next to nothing about eastern religion? In this respect Kierkegaard was very much of his time. (It would be interesting to see what he would have made of the paradoxes of Zen Buddhism, for example, had he lived a century later.) Maybe it is unfair to criticize the narrowness of Kierkegaard's religious outlook, for he does not pretend to be interested in comparative religion, and is quite open about the fact that he is concerned primarily with the distinction between Christians and pseudo-Christians. However, readers who feel dissatisfied with Kierkegaard's account of the religious sphere might want to explore ways in which it could incorporate a broader and more nuanced understanding of different spiritual traditions.

Earlier in this chapter I suggested that the theory of the existential spheres, put together with the claim that subjectivity is truth, is offered as an aid to self-reflection. When we come to evaluate this aspect of Kierkegaard's philosophy, we have to ask ourselves whether the classification of aesthetic, ethical and religious really illuminates our own existence. Personally, I find that all three spheres resonate with my experience, but I certainly do not feel that I have made a clear progression from one to another. On the contrary, I might move between all three within a single day. Is my inconsistency a sign that I am, in fact, an aesthetic person who cannot commit to anything? Or can we challenge the expectation that subjectivities should be consistent: *either* aesthetic, *or* ethical, *or* religious? It is difficult to say whether Kierkegaard intended the spheres to be so clear-cut. And as we have seen, he himself poured all three forms of subjectivity into his authorship – although, according to his own

KIERKEGAARD: A GUIDE FOR THE PERPLEXED

philosophy, we cannot say anything about his religiousness, since whatever reality this had must be purely inward.

Perhaps the most common criticism of Kierkegaard's account of subjectivity – especially in the religious sphere – is that it is too individualistic. This criticism must certainly be taken seriously, and considered carefully. Do the claims that 'subjectivity is truth', and that Christianity is a matter of inwardness, imply that each person pursues her religious life alone before God? Although Kierkegaard is very interested in human relationships, he often handles them quite abstractly, and in his published works he says relatively little about family and friendship. Biographical factors may be relevant here: Kierkegaard had difficult relationships with his father and his brother, and of course he became neither a husband nor a father. On the whole his attitude towards society and the Danish Church is very negative, and it is difficult to establish how much this was due to Kierkegaard's temperament, and how much to philosophical and theological concerns.

On the other hand, we have to take into account the rather modern idea, articulated by Kant and developed by Hegel, that human subjectivity shapes and gives meaning to a world. Understood in this context, Kierkegaard's emphasis on inwardness and his intricate exploration of subjectivity do not imply that the individual is isolated, but show how she relates to the world. He makes this quite explicit in one of his religious discourses, *Strengthening in the Inner Being*, which begins by reflecting on Paul's situation as a prisoner in Rome, and highlighting the contrast between Paul's physical confinement and his spiritual freedom, his inward power. Kierkegaard goes on to distinguish two ways of relating to the world: through knowledge, and through a subjective, passionate 'concern' with questions of meaning. (These correspond to the aesthetic and ethical spheres.) As long as a person is pursuing knowledge, Kierkegaard argues, he 'is indifferent to the world and this world is indifferent through his knowledge of it'. In other words, regarding the truth solely in terms of knowledge brings to light a valueless, meaningless world: knowledge leads to nihilism. When a concern for meaning 'awakens in his soul', the individual finds that he requires a form of truth that goes beyond knowledge: 'This concern . . . craves another kind of knowledge, a knowledge that does not remain as knowledge for a single moment but is transformed into action the moment it is possessed, since otherwise it is not possessed.' This suggests that subjectivity, at least when it develops beyond the aesthetic sphere and becomes more inward, engages with the world and, presumably, with other people. Indeed, the aesthetic person's failure to relate to another's subjectivity is, for Kierkegaard, one of the reasons why this way of life is inadequate.

The reality of another person's subjectivity is a form of objectivity: it is something that exists out there in the world, independent of oneself – and there is a way of relating to other people *as others* that respects their freedom and recognizes their particular needs. This relationship is a 'how' rather than a 'what' (that is, it is subjective) and yet it still requires a certain objectivity. This is not the clinical, detached, indifferent objectivity that Kierkegaard disparages; on the contrary, it is a way of caring for and even loving another person, without being blinded by self-interest and one's own emotions. When one is genuinely concerned for another (and in this case we are already within the ethical or religious sphere), the coolness and clarity of objectivity can help one to see what is best for her. Kierkegaard's view that subjectivity is truth in no way excludes this attitude, because it is rooted in a subjective commitment to act wisely and to help another person. In fact, in his authorship Kierkegaard uses different kinds of objectivity – such as philosophical argument and psychological observation – in order to communicate something that he is passionate about. The claim that subjectivity is truth does not mean that objectivity is untruth: rather, it directs philosophical attention to the ways in which subjectivity can be true or untrue. It may be that an individual is most true to her values and commitments, and indeed to her inner spiritual life, when she makes an effort to be objective about the world, about other people, or about herself.

CHAPTER 5

THE PROBLEM OF SIN

WHAT IS SIN?

From a Christian point of view, any interpretation of human existence has to take into account the idea of sin. Two of Kierkegaard's
pseudonymous texts focus on sin: *The Concept of Anxiety*, by
Vigilius Haufniensis, and *The Sickness Unto Death*, by Anti-
Climacus. The titles of these books alone are enough to frighten
readers new to Kierkegaard, and their content is especially challenging for those unfamiliar with the theological doctrines of original sin and atonement. Many modern readers have little
understanding of what sin actually means, and find the concept to
be quite alien and rather negative and off-putting. From a philosophical point of view it is difficult even to approach the issue of sin,
since it is essentially a sectarian, dogmatic category – that is, it is part
of a particular religious doctrine, and does not have a clear rational
basis. The belief that we are all sinners is not the result of a process
of reasoning, but a fundamental presupposition: as Kierkegaard
puts it in his journals, 'That I exist was the eternal presupposition of
the ancient world: that I am a sinner is the new spontaneity of the
Christian consciousness; the one can be demonstrated no more than
the other.'[1] Even for those who have a background in Christianity,
sin is a complex notion that can be interpreted in various different
ways. And as the history of Christian theology shows, the doctrine
of original sin raises some thorny philosophical questions, and over
the centuries has been the source of much controversy. Furthermore,
as we shall see – and as we may, by now, have come to expect –
Kierkegaard approaches the question of sin in an unusual and original way.

Before we turn to Kierkegaard's analysis of sin, it will be useful to reflect on the notion of sin more generally. People who are unfamiliar with the concept of sin sometimes regard it in moral terms, assuming that it refers to actions that are morally wrong. It is certainly true that immoral actions are expressions of sin, but sin is a much broader term that belongs to religious discourse rather than to morality alone. Put most simply, sin means being in a wrong relationship to God. This means that interpretations of sin can vary according to what is believed to be a *right* relationship to God. For example, from a Jewish point of view this relationship is understood primarily in terms of the law that God, through Moses, revealed to the people of Israel, and so righteousness means obeying the law and sin means transgressing it. Christianity, on the other hand, focuses on love and faith, and this means that (for instance) failing to love one's neighbour as oneself, or to practise forgiveness unconditionally, is a form of sin. This distinction between Judaism and Christianity is of course extremely crude, but it highlights the way in which the relationship between God and human beings provides the context for the concept of sin.

Being in a right relationship to God does not simply mean doing what He tells us, whether this commandment takes the form of a set of laws or a direction to open up one's heart. It also means recognizing fully that God is the source of all things, including oneself – that He is the creator of the world, the giver of life – and honouring this recognition of one's dependence on God by means of worship, gratitude and humility. For this reason attitudes such as pride, complacency and arrogance are sinful, because they demonstrate a lack of respect for God and an ignorance about one's own position in relation to Him. In fact, asserting one's independence from God in any way at all is a form of sin. If we regard our own lives as gifts from God, then even actions that harm only ourselves can be considered sinful, because this kind of behaviour damages or wastes something that ultimately belongs to God.

If sin is essentially a religious concept that must be understood with reference to God, does this mean that it is simply irrelevant for anybody who does not believe in God? As it happens, Kierkegaard's discussion of sin will offer an answer to this question by showing the connections between the psychological experiences of anxiety and despair, and the theological or dogmatic concept of sin. Independently of Kierkegaard, however, it is possible to suggest ways of thinking about sin in more naturalistic, human terms, rather than solely in relation to a supernatural, divine power. After all, everyone lives in relationship to others: we all belong to a larger whole, such as a family, a community and an eco-system, and in different ways we are dependent on these for our existence. Sin could be reinterpreted as a failure to honour this dependence, and an attempt to act as if we were each self-sufficient. Or we might regard sin in terms of a wrong relationship to ourselves, as falling short of what we know to be our potential, or as neglecting an ideal that we hold to be central to our lives. If we take either of these views of sin we are sure to find that, just as Christianity teaches, we are all sinners, and that in fact we fall into sin on a very regular basis.

The Christian concept of sin is intimately connected to the concepts of repentance and forgiveness. Repentance means recognizing one's sinfulness, taking responsibility for it, and resolving to make an effort not to sin again. This is not some sort of optimistic promise, for a little self-knowledge tells us that we *will* sin again, and again, and again. In spite of this, the intention to do one's best and not just surrender to sin is an essential aspect of faith. The inevitability of sin means that it is important to ask for forgiveness, since this is the only way to lighten the burden of guilt that comes with awareness of sin. Even from a non-religious point of view, asking to be forgiven and offering forgiveness to others has a very powerful effect because it makes people feel less burdened by miserable, debilitating feelings such as guilt, shame, anger and bitterness. It is possible to regard sin in terms of imperfect mental health – which, understood broadly, applies to more or less everyone – and to believe that forgiveness brings greater well-being, peace of mind and happiness.

Christianity teaches that we were originally created in the image of God and enjoyed a harmonious relationship to Him. The story of Adam and Eve is used to explain how we fell from this state of perfection to our present, sinful condition: when Adam disobeyed God and ate the fruit from the tree of knowledge, sin first entered the world, became a part of human nature, and corrupted our relationship to God. This story emphasizes that sin was not created by God, but rather by man's assertion of his own will against the will of God. According to the biblical story, we are all descendants of Adam, and therefore we all share in his sinful nature (there are various theories about precisely how Adam's sin is transmitted to each individual). This does not just mean that we all sometimes sin, but that we are all fundamentally sinful, and that therefore we are constantly in need of forgiveness. This is what the doctrine of original sin means. Sometimes this view of humanity seems rather negative and pessimistic, but it can also promote tolerance, compassion and forgiveness by emphasizing that sinfulness is something we all share, something we all experience.

The problem of reconciling the idea that our sinful nature is inherited with the idea that we are each responsible for our sins has generated an ongoing debate between theologians. Some versions of the doctrine of original sin allow the individual a degree of freedom to overcome sin by suggesting that only certain aspects of human nature – such as the body and its desires – are corrupted by it. Both St Augustine and Luther oppose this view by insisting that human beings are thoroughly sinful and are thus unable to free themselves from sin by their own efforts. Kierkegaard's exploration of sin contributes to this theological debate, as well as illuminating the subjective experience of being a sinner.

Kierkegaard's understanding of sin follows the Augustinian–Lutheran tradition in emphasizing that all the capacities of a human being – sensual desire, rational thought, imagination, emotions, the will – are affected by sin. This means that there is no untainted aspect of human nature which is able to overcome and purify the rest, and that therefore we can turn only to God for relief from sinfulness. Kierkegaard's main concern is not to challenge the interpretation of sin that is offered by Augustine and Luther, but to present it in a way that allows the individual to understand her sinfulness more clearly. In his journals Kierkegaard writes that, 'on the whole, the doctrine as it is presented is quite correct. I have no quarrel with it. My contention is that something should be made of it.'[2] It seems that this task of 'making something of sin' means exploring its significance from the perspective of the existing individual. Kierkegaard's point is that although, according to Christian doctrine, we all have to accept that we are sinners through and through, this does not mean that we need not become more intimately acquainted with the way in which we each experience and express our sinfulness subjectively.

One of the confusing things about the view that human beings are sinners is that there are two aspects to sin. On the one hand, sin is an enduring state or condition of human nature, and on the other hand sins are particular actions. Are we sinners because we do sinful things? (Or, in other words, is it our sinful acts that produce the state of being sinful?) Or do we do sinful things because we have sinful natures? Which comes first, the condition of being a sinner, or the particular act of sinning? This question is important because in the case of committing sinful acts we can recognize that the individual has some freedom to choose whether or not to act that way, and can therefore be held responsible for her sins, whereas in the case of being in a state of sin the possibility of choice is less apparent. Some commentators accuse Kierkegaard of holding two contradictory views of sin, because he emphasizes that human nature is completely mired in the state of sin, and that we are unable to overcome this by our own efforts – but he also insists that through our actions we continually, freely bring sin into being.

When it comes to the issue of sin, a certain tension between Kierkegaard's theological and philosophical positions becomes apparent. Theologically, he is quite conservative, and he certainly does not want to challenge the dogmatic claim that we are all sinners; as we have seen, he regards this as a basic presupposition of the Christian life. From a philosophical perspective, however, Kierkegaard's view that existence is dynamic and free, always in the process of becoming, makes him uncomfortable with the idea that a fixed, enduring state can be attributed to human being. There is also a tension between Kierkegaard's philosophical tendency to focus on 'the single individual', and the theological notion of collective, inherited sinfulness. Kierkegaard's approach to sin is shaped by his concern to maintain these different positions simultaneously.

THE CONCEPT OF ANXIETY: THE PSYCHOLOGY OF SIN

The Concept of Anxiety carries the imposing subtitle 'A Simple Psychologically Orienting Deliberation on the Dogmatic Issue of Hereditary Sin' – although most readers will agree that this book is anything but simple. It begins by setting out a clear distinction between dogmatics (the formulation of theological doctrine) and psychology, and by arguing that these cannot be incorporated into a single system. Dogmatics and psychology are two different 'sciences', two distinct spheres, two separate discourses, and each has its own 'mood'. Mixing up these moods and discourses, and attempting to transfer a concept from one to the other, will cause confusion.

For dogmatics, sin is a presupposition that cannot be reduced to any other form of explanation: the doctrine of original sin responds to the question, 'why do people sin?' by stating that we are all sinners. 'Above all, every science must vigorously lay hold of its own beginning and not live in complicated relations with other sciences. If dogmatics wants to begin by explaining sinfulness or by wanting to prove its actuality, no dogmatics will come out of it, but the entire existence of dogmatics will become problematic and vague.'[3] Kierkegaard – or, at least, the pseudonym Vigilius Haufniensis – argues that dogmatics is unable to explain *how* each individual *becomes* a sinner. In other words, dogmatics tells us that the state or condition of sin is ubiquitous and absolute, but it cannot provide a causal explanation for this. In this respect Kierkegaard differs from Augustine and Luther, who put forward doctrines that do not merely state that everyone is a sinner, but also account for each individual's sinfulness by claiming that Adam's sin has been transmitted biologically to all his descendants. For Kierkegaard, this amounts to a deterministic explanation that undermines the fact that we must each take responsibility for our sins, and does not help individuals to understand the roots of sin within themselves.

According to *The Concept of Anxiety*, the dogmatic doctrine of original sin cannot provide an *explanation* for human sinfulness. However, it does provide us with a certain self-understanding: it tells us to view ourselves as sinners, and to view our sinful actions as absolutely typical manifestations of an innate sinfulness (rather than as exceptions to a normal state of goodness or at least neutrality). It also tells us that we are constantly in need of forgiveness. This dogmatic presupposition of sin gives us a kind of clarity and certainty about our situation, and it also offers guidance about how to live – it directs us to be humble, to ask for forgiveness, and shows us that we should never be self-satisfied, proud or complacent. Furthermore, it highlights the individual's bond with the race as a whole: just as our sinful actions reveal the truth about our own natures, so the sins of others also reveal the truth about ourselves. In fact, every particular sin manifests the sinfulness of humanity in general.

For Kierkegaard, the absolute, unconditional nature of the doctrine of original sin has practical benefits. This idea is present in his authorship from its very beginning: the pastor's sermon at the end of *Either/Or* reflects on the themes of justice and sin-consciousness, and insists that the thought that 'in relation to God one is always in the wrong' is edifying and empowering. Usually, of course, we like to be in the right, and find that the experience of being in the wrong is very uncomfortable. However, the pastor suggests that when we truly love another (whether this other is human or divine), finding fault with him or her does not make us happy. We wish to admire, not to blame the loved one – for our own love suffers as a result of this blame. Wanting to be in the right is an assertion of the ego that makes love more difficult and painful; becoming religious involves surrendering this egotistical, defensive sense of self so that compassionate love flows out unhindered. As the pastor says, the desire to be in the wrong 'has its source in your whole being' and 'springs from the love within you'. Without the absolute sense of being *always* in the wrong before God – which is another way of formulating the doctrine of original sin – we would find ourselves trying to calculate the extent to which we are in the wrong and the extent to which we are in the right; the extent to which we are sinners and the extent to which we are righteous. This is indeed the way we judge ourselves in relation to other human beings – but these calculations need to take into account many different factors, are continually subject to revision, and can never arrive at a certain, conclusive judgement. There is always room for doubt. And, claims the pastor, 'when a man is in doubt, he has no power to act'. Doubt is paralysing, and it certainly does not provide a firm basis for action. On the other hand, the unconditional, unambiguous claim to be *always* in the wrong before God releases the individual from the paralysis of doubt: it is 'an animating thought' that 'makes a man glad to act . . . it encourages and inspires to action'.

So, according to Kierkegaard the dogmatic doctrine of original sin provides a basis for the individual's life, although it does not actually explain sin. From this starting-point it is possible to explore sin psychologically and to investigate how particular sinful actions arise. Whereas dogmatics simply states that people sin because they are sinners, psychology can begin to explain sin through careful observation and analysis of the subjectivity of the sinner. Here, as elsewhere, Kierkegaard uses the psychological 'mood' of observation in a religious context in order to promote greater self-understanding, which will lead in turn to deeper repentance. In *The Concept of Anxiety* the pseudonym Vigilius Haufniensis (whose name means 'watchman of Copenhagen') carries out an intricate examination of different psychological states, and suggests that sinful acts come into being from an underlying state of anxiety. In other words, he suggests that anxiety is a psychological state that predisposes us to sin. In this context anxiety is not simply a mood or an emotion that certain people experience at certain times, but a basic response to freedom that is part of the human condition. For Kierkegaard, this investigation of anxiety replaces theological speculation about inherited sinfulness, and illuminates the roots of the individual's experience of temptation in a way that these traditional doctrines do not.

This analysis of anxiety, like the doctrine of original sin, focuses on the story of Adam's first sin. But whereas theologians like Augustine and Luther regard Adam's sinful act as the *cause* of every subsequent person's sinful condition, Kierkegaard treats the story of Adam as a *paradigm*, an example, of every sinner's action. He emphasizes that there is no essential difference between the way in which Adam's sin comes into being and the way in which all other sins come into being – all are equally new, all are equally free, and everyone is equally accountable. In traditional Christian theology, the doctrine of original sin separates Adam, and his sinfulness, from the rest of the human race, by claiming that Adam's sin springs from a state of innocence, whereas all other sins arise from sinfulness that is already there. On this view, our sinfulness is different from Adam's because we inherited it, whereas he brought it into being. On the contrary, says Vigilius Haufniensis, we all repeatedly bring sin into being, just as Adam did in the Garden of Eden: 'Through the first sin, sin came into the world. Precisely the same is true of every subsequent man's first sin, that through it sin comes into the world . . . As the history of the race moves on, the individual continually begins anew . . . Just as Adam lost innocence by guilt, so every man loses it in the same way.'[4]

This means that the story of Adam's sin reveals the motivations of all sin. Vigilius Haufniensis suggests that the psychological condition of anxiety develops when the self emerges from a state of innocence. In this context, innocence means a kind of unreflective unity with one's physical and social environment. According to the biblical story, when God first created the world everything was as it should be: there were no questions to ask, no decisions or value-judgements to be made. Everything was complete, nothing was missing. In other words, Adam and Eve, like all the other creatures in the Garden of Eden, did not have a sense that things could be other than they actually were – they had no sense of *possibility*. Adam and Eve were not ashamed of their nakedness because no other possibility occurred to them.

This idea of possibility is closely connected to language. While God is creating the world, there is no gap between language and reality: everything God says is immediately brought into being ('God said, "Let there be light", and there was light', and so on), or otherwise God gives names to what he has just created. The only exception is God's command that Adam should *not* eat from the tree of knowledge of good and evil, and as we shall see it is this negative statement that leads to the opening up of possibility. Even when Adam speaks for the first time – and until this point God has done all the talking – he simply gives names to his fellow creatures, ending with woman, who is so called 'because she was taken out of man'. The first time that language deviates from actuality is when the serpent asks Eve, 'Did God say, "You shall not eat of any tree of the garden"?' This is the first question in the Hebrew Bible. The serpent's question, like all questions, raises a possibility: it introduces the idea that things might be different from how they actually are. Of course, the serpent knows exactly what God said, but his question suggests to Eve that there is an alternative to God's commandment. It is possibility that awakens desire, for if we had no sense that something was missing, or that our situation could be otherwise, then we would not be capable of desire. Eve tells the serpent that God has forbidden them to eat from the tree in the middle of the garden, for if they do so they will die. 'You will not die', replies the serpent. His first utterance was a question; his second is a contradiction, and this presents Eve with a more concrete possibility – with a choice between accepting the word of God, and accepting the word of the serpent.

The first sin arises out of the situation of possibility, choice, freedom, desire. All of these, suggests Vigilius Haufniensis, create anxiety, because they represent a kind of nothingness, a lack of determination. Haufniensis compares anxiety with the dizziness one feels when looking down into an abyss: 'anxiety is the dizziness of freedom'.[5] When we face the future, we face emptiness and uncertainty. Although anxiety sounds like a wholly negative response, it is, says Vigilius Haufniensis, profoundly ambivalent, because our freedom simultaneously attracts us and repels us. On the one hand, the future is full of possibilities, and this is exciting and appealing, but on the other hand the uncertainty of our future makes us want to cling on to the security of the present. We respond to the future with both hope and fear, and indeed the oscillation between these states intensifies anxiety ('will it be ok? won't it be ok?', 'it's going to be ok! it's not going to be ok!'), because hope and fear are themselves further, more internalized possibilities. When we act, we try to overcome our anxiety by eliminating the uncertainty that possibility presents us with, but of course every new act merely changes the range of possibilities and the abyss of freedom remains as open as before.

From Kierkegaard's point of view, Adam is like everyone else insofar as he is an existing individual who also belongs to and represents the human race as a whole. (And after all, 'Adam' is the Hebrew word for 'human being'.) Adam's experience of sinning reveals the universal situation of freedom, and the universal response of anxiety. The 'science' of dogmatics does not deal with human freedom, for it 'explains' particular acts of sin as manifestations of an innate, enduring condition. Psychology, however, takes a different view of the relationship between the state of being sinful and the act of committing sins: the state is our enduring freedom, the continual presence of possibility, and particular acts are our free responses to this. The story of Adam's first sin is a revelation of man's true nature, and this is the case whether we look at it from a dogmatic or from a psychological standpoint: as dogmatics asserts, we are all sinners, and as psychology discovers, we all fall into sin through anxiety.

Human beings are anxious, says Vigilius Haufniensis, not simply because of their freedom, but because they are a combination of the finite and the infinite, or the limited and the unlimited. Insofar as we are aware of possibilities, and face a future that lacks determination, we are unlimited or infinite, but of course we are also limited by our own particular existence – by our body, our intellect, our environment, and so on. Animals are merely finite, and therefore they are not anxious; God is infinite, unlimited, and therefore He is not anxious either. Vigilius Haufniensis suggests that man's capacity for anxiety is a sign of his spiritual nature: 'If a human being were a beast or an angel, he could not be in anxiety. Because he is a synthesis, he can be in anxiety; and the more profoundly he is in anxiety, the greater is the man.'[6] Here the pseudonym adds that even Jesus felt anxious during the hours before his betrayal by Judas, which was to lead to his death, and he reflects that this suffering in anticipation of something that was about to happen must have been even greater that the suffering of actually being crucified.

In a sense, there is no solution to anxiety, because we are unable to change the fact that our lives, although inevitably limited, also include the dimension of possibility. We cannot escape from anxiety and the suffering it brings. According to Vigilius Haufniensis, the most we can do is bear our anxiety and gain wisdom from this. Particular sinful acts are an attempt – which is always futile – to escape from anxiety, to put 'something' in the place of 'nothing', to crush possibility with a concrete action. This means that the only way to restrain ourselves from committing sins is to endure the anxiety rather than try to flee from it:

> Every human being must . . . learn to be anxious in order that he might not perish either by never having been in anxiety or by succumbing in anxiety. Whoever has learned to be anxious in the right way has learnt the ultimate . . . Whoever is educated by possibility remains with anxiety; he does not permit himself to be deceived by its countless falsifications and accurately remembers the past. Then the assaults of anxiety, even though they be terrifying, will not be such that he flees from them. For him, anxiety will be a serving spirit that against its will leads him where he wishes to go.[7]

At the end of *The Concept of Anxiety*, Vigilius Haufniensis suggests that through anxiety one may reach faith – that, in fact, faith lies only on the far side of anxiety. This echoes the view that we find in *Fear and Trembling*, where faith is shown to come into being only on the basis of great suffering and struggle. Faith is salvation from anxiety – 'in no other place can we find rest' – but it is reached *through* anxiety. Vigilius Haufniensis does not say much about faith itself, but he indicates that it relates to the Christian doctrine of atonement, whereby Jesus's death reconciles man and God, restoring harmony to the relationship that has been out of joint since man's very first sin. (This doctrine is rather obscure, and theologians have offered different explanations of how reconciliation is actually accomplished through Jesus, just as they have proposed various theories of original sin.) Faith and atonement are beyond the boundaries of psychology, for they belong to dogmatics, and this is why the pseudonym ends his discussion at this point: 'as soon as psychology has finished with anxiety, it is to be delivered to dogmatics'. Having limited his investigation to the sphere of psychology, Vigilius Haufniensis is unable to explain how anxiety can be transformed into faith.

THE SICKNESS UNTO DEATH: SIN AND DESPAIR

The Sickness Unto Death was published in 1849, five years after *The Concept of Anxiety*. There are certainly similarities between the two texts: they both deal with sin, and they both present a detailed exploration of the psychological experiences associated with being a sinner: while the first focuses on anxiety, the second examines despair. This highlights another common theme: the connection between sin and suffering. Kierkegaard does not present suffering as a consequence of sin, as some kind of punishment for it, but rather as a state that inevitably accompanies sin – as a kind of symptom of the spiritual 'sickness' that is our sinful condition. An important difference between the books, however, is that *The Sickness Unto Death* places much more emphasis on the individual's relationship to God. As we have seen, sin itself is defined in terms of this relationship, but *The Concept of Anxiety* concentrates on the way in which sin arises from an experience of possibility: even though God is certainly present in the story of Adam's first sin, the aspect of this story that most interests Vigilius Haufniensis is the way that it exemplifies the human response to freedom. The pseudonym Anti-Climacus, on the other hand, considers sin from an explicitly Christian point of view. The subtitle of *The Sickness Unto Death* makes Anti-Climacus's religious intentions very clear: 'A Christian Psychological Exposition for Upbuilding and Awakening'.

The Sickness Unto Death is divided into two parts, and the concept of sin is not introduced until the second part. Part One, 'The Sickness Unto Death is Despair', investigates the experience of despair and discusses several different forms of despair. Although Anti-Climacus does not here make any reference to sin, the book begins with a description of the self that fits in with the traditional definition of sin as the disruption of man's relationship to God. 'The self is a relation that relates itself to itself', suggests Anti-Climacus; 'a human being is a synthesis of the infinite and the finite, of the temporal and the eternal, of freedom and necessity, in short, a synthesis. A synthesis is a relation between two. Considered in this way, a human being is still not a self.' A human being is already a relation, a synthesis, but this synthesis only becomes a self when it relates itself to itself, or in other words when it becomes aware of itself. Anti-Climacus then points out that a self 'must either have established itself or have been established by another', and suggests that a human self is 'a derived, established relation . . . that . . . in relating itself to itself relates itself to another'.[8] This sounds very complicated, because the pseudonym uses such abstract language, but basically the point is that the human self owes its existence to God, and therefore only becomes itself – becomes what it really is – through relating to God. A self is not something independent or ready-made that can either relate to God or exist alone; rather a self is *in essence* a relationship to God. Regarding the human self in this way means that a problem within the self – such as despair – is really a problem in the individual's relationship to God, or, in other words, sin. Despair is different from anxiety because it is always, in fact, before God. Anxiety is a response to the tension between the finite and infinite aspects of human existence, whereas despair results from the way the self as a whole is in some sense untrue to its wholeness. Whilst anxiety is a symptom of poor mental or emotional health, despair is a symptom of poor spiritual health.

Anti-Climacus begins by describing despair without explicit reference to God or to sin. This gives the reader a chance to identify with the experience of despair on a purely psychological level. But, when in Part Two the reader learns that 'Despair Is Sin', she is more likely to recognize that she is indeed a sinner, and this will awaken a willingness to seek the remedy of faith. As the subtitle of the book indicates, its purpose is 'upbuilding and awakening', and it points out a path leading from despair to faith as freedom from despair.

There are two important aspects of Anti-Climacus's analysis of despair and sin that need to be emphasized. In fact, these are connected with one another. The first is that, as we have seen, Anti-Climacus presents the whole subject as a matter of sickness and health: despair, he says, is a sickness of the spirit. This medical metaphor runs through the text, and the pseudonym uses it to make the point that just as individuals are not well qualified to assess their own physical state of health, so they are not experts in their own spiritual health. This means that it is possible for people to be in despair without realizing it, or to think that they are in despair without really understanding the nature of the condition. In fact, both of these attitudes are forms of self-deception which are them-selves types of despair. In the first case, people who do not think they are in despair are not conscious that anything is wrong with their relationship to God – perhaps because they do not even recognize that they *have* this relationship – and this ignorance is a very grave defect in their relationship to God. In the second case, people confuse states such as misery and inner conflict with despair, and again their confusion and ignorance is itself symptomatic of despair.

> As a rule, a person is supposed to be healthy when he himself does not say that he is sick, not to mention when he himself says that he is well. But the physician has a different view of sickness. Why? Because the physician has a defined and developed conception of what it is to be healthy, and ascertains a man's condition accord-ingly. The physician knows that just as there is merely imaginary sickness so there is also merely imaginary health, and in the latter case he first takes measures to disclose the sickness. Generally speaking, the physician, precisely because he is a physician (well informed), does not have complete confidence in what a person says about his condition . . . A physician's task is not only to pre-scribe remedies but also, first and foremost, to identify the sick-ness, and consequently his first task is to ascertain whether the supposedly sick person is actually sick or whether the supposedly healthy person is perhaps actually sick. Such also is the relation of the physician of the soul to despair.[9]

It is clear that Anti-Climacus's role here is that of 'physician of the soul'. As we saw in Chapter 2, Kierkegaard regarded Anti-Climacus as more Christian than himself, and one of the pseudonym's func-tions is to be someone who is well qualified to treat the sickness of despair – because he knows what it is to be healthy, or, in other words, he knows what it is to have faith. Kierkegaard himself would not have been comfortable with making such a claim.

Anti-Climacus's vocabulary of health and sickness is important for a number of reasons. It explains the structure of the text, which follows the physician's method of first diagnosing and explaining the nature of the sickness before offering a cure. *The Sickness Unto Death* begins with despair and ends with faith. The analogy between an undiscovered illness and an unacknowledged despair implies that self-deception can be very dangerous, and this encourages readers to look at themselves more closely and with more honesty. The medical metaphor also suggests that the 'prescription' of faith is for the individual's own benefit: it is for the sake of alleviating the painful condition of despair, rather than a moralizing demand that the reader 'ought' to have faith in order to be a 'good' person. The language of health and sickness is morally neutral, and Anti-Climacus emphasizes that 'the opposite of sin is not virtue but faith'.[10] This means that sin is associated with a lack of wholeness and harmony, rather than with a notion of evil. The term 'sickness' also highlights the suffering that sin involves, so that restoring the relationship to God through faith offers happiness and not merely righteousness. This emphasis on suffering encourages a compassionate rather than a judgemental response to the sinfulness of others, which is very much in line with Jesus's own teaching.

The second important aspect of Anti-Climacus's analysis of despair and sin is that he makes it very clear that these are conditions of the will. This means that even though despair seems inevitable, it is a state that we must accept responsibility for – and this echoes Vigilius Haufniensis' argument in *The Concept of Anxiety*. Outlining the different forms of despair in Part One of the book, Anti-Climacus identifies two basic kinds of despair: 'in despair not to will to be oneself', or 'despair in weakness', and 'in despair to will to be oneself', or 'defiance'. Weakness and defiance are both qualities of the will. People who suffer from the weak form of despair do not feel strong enough to live their lives in relation to God, and remain within a merely human, worldly existence. Even if these people understand that there is more to life than this, they only despair of their failure to realize a more spiritual life. Those who are defiantly in despair resist any help and prefer to hold on to their suffering; they would rather be 'themselves' as they are, in despair, than risk losing this identity:

A sufferer usually has one or several ways in which he might want to be helped. If he is helped in these ways, then he is glad to be helped. But when having to be helped becomes a profoundly earnest matter, especially when it means being helped by a superior, or by the supreme one, there is the humiliation of being obliged to accept any kind of help unconditionally, of becoming nothing in the hand of the 'Helper' for whom all things are

possible [here Anti-Climacus is referring to God], or the humiliation of simply having to yield to another person, of giving up
being himself as long as he is seeking help. Yet there is undoubt-
edly much suffering, even prolonged and agonised suffering, in
which the self nevertheless is not pained in this way, and therefore
it fundamentally prefers the suffering along with the retention of
being itself.[11]

This kind of despair is a form of self-assertion, which in the context
of the idea of sin means an unwillingness to acknowledge one's
dependence on God. At the extreme end of defiance is what Anti-
Climacus calls 'demonic despair', which is the 'most intensive' form
of despair:

> In hatred towards existence [this despair] wills to be itself, wills to
> be itself in accordance with its misery. Not even in defiance . . .
> does it will to be itself, but for spite; not even in defiance does it
> want to tear itself loose from the power that established it, but for
> spite wants to force itself upon it . . . Rebelling against all exist-
> ence, it feels that it has obtained evidence against it, its goodness.
> The person in despair believes that he himself is the evidence, and
> that is what he wants to be, and therefore he wants to be himself,
> himself in his torment, in order to protest against all existence
> with this torment. Just as the weak, despairing person is unwill-
> ing to hear anything about any consolation eternity has for him,
> so a person in such despair does not want to hear anything about
> it either, but for a different reason: this consolation would be his
> undoing . . .[12]

Although he makes a clear distinction between weak and defiant
despair, Anti-Climacus also suggests that in practice no despair is
entirely free of either weakness or defiance.

Anti-Climacus's emphasis on the centrality of the will is important because he wishes to draw a contrast between the Christian doctrine of sin, and Socrates' understanding of it. Socrates regards sin
as due to ignorance, and for this reason his teaching focuses on
awakening wisdom: as far as Socrates is concerned, once a person
knows what is right, she will automatically do it. This represents a
fundamental weakness in Socrates' philosophy: it does not take into
account the gap between knowing what is good and actually putting

this into action; a basic fact of life, as anyone who has ever made a New Year's resolution will know very well. From the point of view of Christianity, we have been shown exactly what is right – indeed, God has even revealed Himself in human form, and has taught us to have faith, to repent of our sins, to practise love and forgiveness, and so on. It couldn't be much clearer. However, because sin is a defect of the *will*, it is possible to turn away from this revelation in an unwillingness to understand it, or to understand it and yet wilfully ignore it, forget about it, or reject it.

Anti-Climacus distinguishes between conscious and unconscious despair, but he admits that this is too simplistic to apply to real life, and he suggests that there are many different ways of avoiding despair. Although people in despair almost always have a dim awareness of their condition, they may try to ignore this, or to distract themselves by working or by keeping busy in some other way. This attempt to divert attention from despair implies that people do indeed have some consciousness of it, and yet they may not entirely realize their own motivations for keeping so busy. All of this involves a good deal of self-deception. 'There is indeed in all darkness and ignorance a dialectical interplay between willing and knowing', observes Anti-Climacus.

Even if we do not wilfully turn away from knowledge of the good, and indeed accept the importance of acting upon this knowledge, unless willing follows *immediately* from knowing then the will is defective and sin is still present. And as we all know, human beings are inclined to let things drift for a while. As far as Anti-Climacus is concerned, this is not good enough:

In the life of the spirit there is no standing still . . . therefore, if a person does not do what is right at the very second he knows it – then, first of all, knowing simmers down . . . If willing does not agree with what is known, then it does not necessarily follow that willing goes ahead and does the opposite of what knowing understood (presumably such strong opposites are rare); rather, willing allows some time to elapse, an interim called: 'we shall look at it tomorrow'. During all this, knowing becomes more and more obscure, and the lower nature gains the upper hand more and more; alas, for the good should be done immediately, as soon as it is known, but the inner nature's power lies in stretching things out.[13]

This reflects Kierkegaard's emphasis on becoming, which in the case of sin means that repentance must be active at every moment. According to Anti-Climacus, the continuity of sin arises from ceaseless repetition: 'every unrepented sin is a new sin and every moment that it remains unrepented is also new sin'. Similarly, in order to remain free of despair the self must continually renew its relationship to God, for 'every moment that a self exists, it is in a process of becoming . . . Insofar, then, as the self does not become itself, it is not itself; but not to be itself is precisely despair'.[14]

We might at this point feel tempted to protest that Anti-Climacus is presenting the Christian with an impossibly high ideal to live up to. We might, indeed, find ourselves reacting with either weakness or defiance: 'There's no way I can do that, I give up', or 'Who is this God who demands the impossible? Why should I try at all? I'd rather be in despair!' (This highlights the fact that it is difficult to criticize this text without appearing to exhibit some form of despair – denial, weakness or defiance – and in this way strengthening Anti-Climacus's argument.) Anti-Climacus admits that the Christian teaching about sin is uncompromising, but he also points out that the other side of the teaching – the doctrine of atonement – is just as far beyond human reach. According to the pseudonym, Christianity is 'as paradoxical on this point as possible', because 'it seems to be working against itself by establishing sin so securely as a position that now it seems to be utterly impossible to eliminate it again – and then it is this same Christianity that by means of the Atonement wants to eliminate sin as completely as if it were drowned in the sea'.[15] From Anti-Climacus's point of view, it is absolutely crucial that his readers understand that they are unable to overcome sin through their own efforts, because such self-assertion would only amount to a deeper form of sin. This is why he insists more than once that the opposite of sin is not virtue, but faith. From the very beginning of the book it has been established that the self is dependent on God, and Anti-Climacus emphasizes 'the inability of the self to arrive at or to be in equilibrium and rest by itself'. If the despairing person has become aware of his despair, 'and now with all his power seeks to break his despair by himself and by himself alone – he is still in despair and with all his presumed effort only works himself all the deeper into deeper despair'.[16]

The Sickness Unto Death, like *The Concept of Anxiety*, ends by gesturing towards faith. Anti-Climacus does not say a great deal about faith, but he is a little more forthcoming than Vigilius Haufniensis. Especially interesting is his description of complete freedom from despair: 'in relating itself to itself and in willing to be itself, the self rests transparently in the power that established it'. This appears very near the beginning of Part One, and is repeated right at the end of the book, where Anti-Climacus points out that this also acts as a definition for faith. The phrase 'willing to be itself' here indicates that faith, like sin and despair, is a quality of the will, but in this case the movement is one of self-acceptance rather than self-assertion. 'In relating itself to itself and in willing to be itself' means existing before God with full acceptance of one's dependence on Him. In accepting one's relationship to God, one also accepts oneself – just as a defective relationship to God is always at the same time a sickness within the self.

Perhaps the most striking aspect of Anti-Climacus's description of faith is the image of the self 'resting transparently' in God. This idea of transparency has connotations of purity, emptiness, lightness, receptivity and clarity. Even though the self 'rests' in this state, the fact that existence is always becoming, always a movement, implies that this resting is itself dynamic – and this means that 'resting transparently' involves purifying, emptying, receiving and making clear and light. In faith, the self completely opens itself up to God – to God's power, love, forgiveness and grace, which are actually all the same thing – without any attempt to hide or to resist. Transparency is a kind of self-surrender, led by the will, of the individual's whole being.

More than any other subject, sin illuminates the fascinating interaction between theology, philosophy and psychology within Kierkegaard's thought. In both *The Concept of Anxiety* and *The Sickness Unto Death* a strong ethical individualism, emphasizing freedom and responsibility, comes face to face with an idea of universal and collective sinfulness. A commitment to the perspective of subjectivity comes face to face with the doctrines of atonement and grace, which refer to something completely beyond human power. And a radical, highly original philosophy comes face to face with orthodox Christian theology. Of course, if a conflict emerges between any of these forces, then Kierkegaard will always make philosophy bow down and retreat, admitting the presence of a paradox. But what is most impressive about Kierkegaard's thought is that on the whole he manages to combine these different perspectives. He finds a paradigm of freedom and becoming in the story of Adam and Eve and, entirely consistently with his philosophical position, treats this as the enduring and universal basis of original sin. He shows that sin and suffering belong together, and that both are effects (or defects) of the human will, and yet he refuses to take a moralistic, judgemental stance and appeals instead to divine grace. And he insists that the self freely becoming itself and the individual completely surrendering to God are actually one and the same movement.

CHAPTER 6

FEAR AND TREMBLING: FAITH BEYOND REASON

INTRODUCING THE STORY OF ABRAHAM

In 1849 Kierkegaard wrote in his journal, 'Oh, once I am dead – then *Fear and Trembling* alone will be enough to give me the name of an immortal author: then it will be read and translated into foreign languages. The reader will almost shrink from the frightful pathos in the book.'[1] This private prediction has turned out to be quite accurate: *Fear and Trembling* is one of Kierkegaard's best-known and most widely read books, and its original and provocative interpretation of the biblical story of Abraham and Isaac continues to challenge and unsettle readers. The text delves beneath traditional accounts of Abraham's great faith, and brings out the horrifying and incomprehensible aspects of his story: this man is asked by God to take his son to Mount Moriah and kill him there, and rather than questioning the authenticity of the command, or his own sanity, he immediately obeys. Kierkegaard uses the example of Abraham to examine the relationship between faith and reason, and to undermine Hegel's attempt to incorporate religious faith into a rational system. *Fear and Trembling* also offers profound reflections on the human experiences of love and suffering, and discusses how a religious person can respond to these.

Published in 1843 under the pseudonym Johannes de silentio ('of silence'), *Fear and Trembling* is one of Kierkegaard's earliest works. However, it presents ideas that remain central to his entire authorship: the inwardness of faith, the contradictory nature of God, the difficulty of being authentically religious, the significance of repetition, the importance of movement, the claim of religion to be a sphere of its own beyond both rationality and ethics. Although *Fear and Trembling* focuses on a story from the Hebrew Bible, and makes little explicit reference to Christianity, it presents an interpretation of faith that points to a particular understanding of what it means to become a Christian. This anticipates Kierkegaard's later accounts of Christianity in texts like *Philosophical Fragments*, *Concluding Unscientific Postscript*, *Practice in Christianity*, and the numerous edifying works written in his own name. By drawing attention to the shocking and morally offensive character of Abraham's actions, Kierkegaard tries to disturb the complacent, superficial presumption of faith that he perceives amongst his contemporaries.

All of this takes place in response to Hegelian philosophy, and in particular to its claim that rational thought represents a more complete expression of truth than religious faith. Hegel himself expresses admiration for Abraham, but Kierkegaard argues that this is inconsistent with his philosophy, which claims that the individual finds fulfilment and becomes ethical through participation in a community. According to this view, Abraham cannot be regarded as ethical, or as worthy of praise. More generally, Abraham's faith simply does not make sense, and this excludes him from Hegel's rational system. Kierkegaard suggests it is impossible to admire Abraham unless we accept that there is an alternative to Hegelian values. In effect, he asks the reader to choose: *either* Hegel, *or* Abraham – but not both at once.

The anti-Hegelian intent of *Fear and Trembling* is made clear to the attentive reader in the book's Preface. The pseudonym Johannes de silentio begins by making a comparison between the world of ideas and the world of commerce, and he suggests that in both of these spheres goods are currently being sold 'at a bargain price'. Then he starts to talk about doubt and faith, claiming that people in the academic world are reaching – or presuming to reach – doubt and faith too soon, without the intellectual, emotional and spiritual expenditure that these demand:

> Every speculative monitor who conscientiously signals the import-
> ant trends in modern philosophy, every assistant professor, tutor,
> and student, every rural outsider and tenant incumbent in philoso-
> phy is unwilling to stop with doubting everything but must go
> further . . . They have all made this preliminary movement and pre-
> sumably so easily that they find it unnecessary to say a word about
> *how* . . . how a person is to act in carrying out this enormous task.[2]

The 'speculative monitors' that the pseudonym refers to here are the Hegelian intellectuals whom Kierkegaard had encountered as a student at the University of Copenhagen. He is accusing these Hegelians of setting a 'low price' on faith, by placing it relatively low down on a scale of value that ranks rational thought as the highest form of truth. But faith cannot be fully grasped by the intellect: 'Even if someone were able to transpose the whole content of faith into conceptual form, it does not follow that he has comprehended faith, comprehended how he entered into it or how it entered into him.'[3] Kierkegaard is going to use the story of Abraham to raise the status of faith by showing that it is, in fact, an 'enormous task' and a rare achievement.

At the very end of *Fear and Trembling* the pseudonym returns to his comparison between the world of commerce and the world of ideas. In the book's Epilogue he claims once again that faith is being under-valued in the present age. He suggests that, just as merchants have sunk cargoes of spices in the sea in order to inflate the price of the remaining produce, so a similar sort of measure is needed in the world of ideas to raise the value of faith. The preceding chapters of the book have made it quite clear that Hegelian philosophy has to be 'sunk', or rejected, because it puts forward a scale of value that cannot accommodate the greatness of Abraham's faith.

The Preface and Epilogue of *Fear and Trembling* provide a kind of frame for the rest of the text, clarifying its concern to elevate the value of faith. Kierkegaard's interpretation of the story of Abraham implies that the relative positions of faith and conceptual thought within the Hegelian system need to be reversed. As in *Either/Or*, he relegates intellectual reflection to the lowest, 'aesthetic' level of exist-ence, whilst religious faith is placed even higher than ethics. In the middle of the book Johannes de silentio discusses three Problems that arise from the story of Abraham, and the purpose of each of these is to show that we can admire Abraham only if we recognize a scale of value, or a form of truth, that is quite different from Hegel's theory of mediation. Unless we step outside the Hegelian system, Abraham's actions cannot be justified and we are forced to conclude that he is no better than a murderer. As we shall see, Kierkegaard's alternative scale of value reflects both his account of the three spheres of existence – aesthetic, ethical and religious – and his suggestion that the truth that is essential to human life is characterized by subjective qualities such as fidelity, authenticity, passion and repetition.

According to this scale of value, the pseudonym Johannes de silentio is positioned somewhere between Hegelian philosophy and Abraham. This is reflected in his contrasting attitudes towards them: he *looks up to* Abraham in awe, whereas he *looks down on* Hegelian philosophy rather contemptuously. He suggests that it takes a certain amount of passion to recognize that one does not understand something, and he demonstrates this passion when he remarks that, whilst he has understood Hegelian philosophy fairly well, he is unable to comprehend Abraham:

> I am constantly aware of the prodigious paradox that is the content of Abraham's life, I am constantly repelled and, despite all its passion, my thought cannot penetrate it, cannot get ahead by a hairsbreadth. I stretch every muscle to get a perspective, and at the very same instant I become paralyzed.[4]

The pseudonym's acceptance of his intellectual limitations – and, indeed, of the limitations of intellectual reflection in general when it comes to appreciating Abraham's greatness – is important. It is a sign of his recognition that faith involves a transcendent religious movement, and this makes him existentially 'higher' than Hegelian philosophers, who, according to Kierkegaard, delude themselves in presuming to comprehend faith and to have moved beyond it. Johannes de silentio knows that he falls far short of Abraham's achievement:

> For my part, I presumably can describe the movements of faith, but I cannot make them. In learning to go through the motions of swimming, one can be suspended from the ceiling in a harness and then presumably describe the movements, but one is not swimming. In the same way I can describe the movements of faith.[5]

This distinction between describing movements and making movements highlights the idea that, in order to get beyond the aesthetic sphere of existence, possibilities have to be actualized rather than merely contemplated and explored. Whereas Johannes de silentio, like most of Kierkegaard's narrators, is a commentator on philosophy, psychology, spirituality, and so on, Abraham does not indulge in this sort of reflection. On the contrary, he offers no explanations, remains silent, and simply acts.

Fear and Trembling's Preface is followed by a section entitled 'Exordium', in which Johannes de silentio introduces the story of Abraham from the perspective of someone who is passionately interested in it. This man is not a thinker or a scholar; in other words, he does not approach the story of Abraham objectively. As he grows older he becomes increasingly fascinated by Abraham, but less and less able to understand him. He marvels at Abraham's faith, but he cannot explain it. This presents a challenge to Hegel's view that truth is an historical progression towards greater intellectual clarity: in this case, the individual's understanding seems to diminish as time goes by. Johannes de silentio describes how Abraham's admirer imagines different ways in which Abraham might have responded to the command to sacrifice Isaac. In one scenario he pretends that it is his own wish, not God's, in order to protect Isaac's faith:

> 'Stupid boy, do you think I am your father? I am an idolater. Do you think it is God's command? No, it is my desire.' Then Isaac trembled and cried out in anguish: 'God in heaven, have mercy on me, God of Abraham, have mercy on me; if I have no father on earth, then you be my father!' But Abraham said softly to himself, 'Lord God in heaven, I thank you; it is better that he believes me to be a monster than that he should lose faith in you.'[6]

Alternatively, Abraham decides to sacrifice the ram instead of Isaac, and his faith in God never recovers: 'From that day on, Abraham was old; he could not forget that God had ordered him to do this. Isaac flourished as before, but Abraham's eyes were darkened and he saw joy no more.' In a third version of the story Abraham goes alone to Mount Moriah, where he begs God to forgive him for thinking about killing Isaac, and for forgetting his ethical duty. Another possibility is that Abraham obeys God, but in despair, and this makes Isaac lose his faith:

> Abraham made everything ready for the sacrifice, calmly and gently, but when he turned away and drew the knife, Isaac saw that Abraham's left hand was clenched in despair, that a shudder went through his whole body – but Abraham drew the knife.
>
> Then they returned home again, and Sarah hurried to meet them, but Isaac had lost his faith.[7]

These reactions would be understandable, but what actually happens defies comprehension. Abraham is neither defiant, nor bitter, nor doubtful, nor despairing: he rises early in the morning, eager to set off for Mount Moriah; he is absolutely obedient to God's command, and yet when Isaac asks innocently where they will find something to sacrifice, Abraham replies that 'God will provide' an animal for the offering. How can he believe this when he knows that God wants him to sacrifice Isaac? Surely God would not contradict Himself? In fact, God's command is already contradictory, because before Isaac was born (when Abraham's wife Sarah was ninety years old, and assumed she could not have children) God had promised to make Abraham the father of a nation – and this is what Isaac represents. Doesn't this make it more likely that Abraham is mistaken, rather than God actually wanting him to kill Isaac? How on earth can Abraham's actions be justified?

Reflecting on these questions, Johannes de silentio marvels at Abraham's response to God:

> All was lost! Seventy years of trusting expectancy [before Sarah gave birth to Isaac], the brief joy over the fulfillment of faith . . . Is there no sympathy for this venerable old man, none for the innocent child? And yet Abraham was God's chosen one, and it was the Lord who imposed the ordeal . . . But Abraham had faith and did not doubt; he believed the preposterous. If Abraham had doubted, then he would have . . . gone to Mount Moriah, he would have split the firewood, lit the fire, drawn the knife. He would have cried out to God, 'Reject not this sacrifice; it is not the best that I have, that I know very well, for what is an old man compared to the child of promise, but it is the best I can give you. Let Isaac never find this out so that he may take comfort in his youth'. He would have thrust the knife into his own breast. He would have been admired in the world, and his name would never have been forgotten; but it is one thing to be admired and yet another to become a guiding star that saves the anguished.[8]

This 'Eulogy on Abraham' suggests that Abraham is the father of faith, the first man to show his faith in God's mercy in spite of all evidence to the contrary. Johannes de silentio describes this kind of faith as 'that prodigious passion, that supreme passion'. In places – including this passage above – Kierkegaard seems to be implying that there is a parallel between Abraham and Jesus, for both suffered in their relationships to God and yet maintained their faith in Him.

By presenting the different possibilities that were available to Abraham, Kierkegaard emphasizes the fact that obeying God in the way that he did required a choice, a decision. Abraham was not compelled to sacrifice Isaac: he could have defied God, or he could have submitted to God's will reluctantly, and only outwardly, while despairing in his heart. Reflecting on Abraham's response to God also has the effect of slowing the story down, and directing the reader's attention to the process that leads up to the dramatic climax at the summit of Mount Moriah. Often, says Johannes de silentio, the story is told in such a way that it jumps suddenly from God's command to the moment when Abraham raises his knife over Isaac – and, having proved his obedience, is told that he may sacrifice a ram instead. But what about Abraham's three-day journey to Mount Moriah? How did he feel as he travelled to execute his son? Every step along the way is an expression of Abraham's faith, and of his commitment to God: at each moment he could have stopped, or turned back, and this means that his decision to obey God is renewed continually. Abraham's journey provides a concrete illustration of Kierkegaard's concept of repetition, since each step forward marks a repetition of faith. In this way faith gains a constancy through time: not by standing still, but by a movement of becoming.

We will examine the nature of Abraham's faith in more detail when we turn to later sections of *Fear and Trembling*. For now, we need to take note of the way in which Abraham exemplifies the qualities of authenticity, honesty and fidelity that, as we saw in Chapter 4, characterize the existential, subjective form of truth which Kierkegaard values more highly than objective knowledge. 'What did Abraham achieve? He remained true to his love', writes Johannes de silentio. This highlights an extremely important aspect of Kierkegaard's thought: as a philosopher of Christianity, he is concerned to elucidate the kind of truth that belongs to love, rather than the kind of truth that belongs to knowledge. Knowledge is true if it is correct, if it reflects a conformity between what is thought and what is real; love is true if it is sincere, deep and faithful, and if it endures even through difficult times. For Kierkegaard, the essence of Christianity is that this truth is not only higher than intellectual knowledge, but higher than the ethical law. Although Abraham is not, of course, a Christian, he remains true to his love for God through the most difficult situation imaginable – and this, according to Kierkegaard, raises him above the ethical sphere.

But what about Abraham's love for Isaac? Does his willingness to kill his son mean that he fails to be true to *this* love? From Kierkegaard's point of view, the answer has to be no, for two reasons. First, it is Abraham's love for Isaac that testifies to his love for God: the fact that he is prepared to give up what is most precious to him shows that his faith is authentic. If Abraham did not care about Isaac, then sacrificing him would be meaningless; he gives up everything for God, precisely because Isaac means everything to him. In this way, the story of Abraham illustrates the common religious idea – which becomes particularly prevalent in Christianity – that the individual must surrender herself in order to enter into a relationship with God. In Abraham's case, this means renouncing Isaac, since his son's life is more valuable to him than his own. The second reason why Abraham does not betray Isaac is that he continues to believe that Isaac will live – because he still trusts in God's promise that he will be the father of a nation. At no point does Abraham's love for God *or* for his son waver: he remains absolutely true to his love. Even if God had not stopped him from killing Isaac, Abraham would presumably have carried on believing that Isaac would somehow be returned to him. Of course, this may not seem to provide much consolation for Isaac, but Kierkegaard makes no attempt to lighten the appalling, morally reprehensible character of Abraham's action. His point is not that what Abraham did is acceptable, but, on the contrary, that he proved his faith by doing something that is absolutely unacceptable. In this way Kierkegaard emphasizes the difficulty and rarity of faith: the 'fear and trembling' that tends to be forgotten in the comfort of a bourgeois Christian household.

RESPONDING TO SUFFERING: RESIGNATION AND FAITH

The main body of the text consists of three questions concerning the legitimacy of Abraham's actions. These 'Problemata' (Problems) are prefaced by a 'Preliminary Expectoration', which literally means an introduction that is 'coughed up', 'coming from the chest', or from the heart. In this important section Johannes de silentio discusses the nature of faith, emphasizing that it grows out of an encounter

with suffering. Kierkegaard's point here is that faith is not an immediate, naive, childlike state, but a mature and courageous response to
a painful experience. He suggests that faith involves a kind of leap
(because it is a movement from one form of existence to another,
fundamentally different one), and he uses the metaphor of a ballet
dancer to illustrate this. The dancer's leap looks smooth and easy,
but the apparent lightness of her movement is actually due to the
years of dedicated practice that have strengthened her muscles and
toughened her feet. The same is true of faith: it might look easy and
spontaneous to an outsider, but it is possible only because of the
individual's consistent struggle to confront and to bear with the
difficulties of existence.

In discussing the religious person's response to the suffering that
is an inevitable part of human life, Johannes de silentio revives an
ancient question that continues to challenge defenders of religious
faith: how can we believe in a loving, all-powerful God when there
is so much misery and injustice in the world that He is supposed to
have created? This idea that the manifest presence of affliction and
wrongdoing conflicts with belief in God is often called 'the problem
of evil'. Many philosophers and theologians have attempted to
resolve this problem, by somehow reconciling human suffering with
the existence of God. For Kierkegaard, however, the religious
person's task is not to reconcile or to avoid this contradiction, but to
continue to have faith in full awareness of it.

In order to grasp the significance and originality of Kierkegaard's
position, we need to consider how it differs from the way in which
the most influential philosophers of his day, Kant and Hegel,
address the 'problem of evil'. Kant recognizes fully that moral
justice is lacking in the world – that virtuous people often suffer,
while selfish people flourish. It is precisely for this reason, argues
Kant, that we have to believe in a just God, and in an afterlife in
which the good will be rewarded and the wicked punished. This provides a kind of guarantee that our ethical pursuit of the highest good
(which Kant defines as the conjunction of virtue *and* happiness) is
realistic, and therefore justified. Kant claims that it is rational to
believe in God *because* worldly justice is inevitably flawed. Hegel, on
the other hand, argues that history is progressing in the direction of
a concrete reconciliation between God and the world, which will
narrow the gap between divine perfection and worldly imperfection,
and finally resolve the contradiction altogether. Although Kant and

Hegel offer quite different responses to the 'problem of evil', they both establish our connection to God through reason. In this way, our claim upon God – that human existence should make sense, both intellectually and morally – is secured as rational. They both try to argue that we can expect justice and happiness eventually, so that the 'problem of evil' is only relative and temporary.

Kierkegaard approaches the 'problem of evil' quite differently. He emphasizes the contradiction between the belief that God is good, and the ubiquitous experience of suffering. His pseudonym Johannes de silentio suggests that, instead of attempting to secure and to justify her claims upon existence, the religious person needs to renounce them. This will mean that she stops chasing after the worldly things that she thinks will bring her satisfaction, and instead focuses on her relationship to God. The most extreme form of this renunciation is the monastic life. Renouncing her claim upon the finite world enables the religious individual to love God purely and wholeheartedly: 'what I gain in resignation is my eternal conscious-ness . . . my eternal consciousness is my love for God'.[9] Johannes de silentio calls this religious act 'infinite resignation', and he describes the person who accomplishes it as a 'knight of resignation'.

The knight of resignation responds to the contradiction between his experience of the world and his belief in God by giving up the expectation that happiness and justice *should* be features of the world. He accepts that the finite world and the spiritual world are simply incommensurable, and he turns his attentions entirely to the spiritual world:

> Spiritually speaking, everything is possible, but in the world of the finite there is much that is not possible. This impossibility, however, the knight makes possible by waiving his claim to it. The wish [for happiness and satisfaction] which would carry him out into actuality, but has been stranded on impossibility, is now turned inward, but it is not therefore lost, nor is it forgotten.[10]

This detachment from earthly things offers a certain consolation, and helps the knight of resignation to bear the painful reality of life. It is important to note that this is not an avoidance of suffering, but an acceptance of it: 'the knight will recollect everything, but this rec-ollection is precisely the pain'. We should also bear in mind that although resignation accomplishes a kind of peace and rest within

the soul, this repose is maintained only if the movement of resignation is repeated continually. This is why the religious person requires
strength and passion – a sort of spiritual energy that underlies the
constancy of his love for God. In fact, Johannes de silentio suggests
that resignation expresses all of a person's power: 'I continually use
my strength in resigning everything . . . I use all my strength in
resigning.'[11]

In this context, passion bears its full meaning, which includes
both love and suffering. The knight of resignation accepts suffering
in order to love God wholeheartedly. He does not lose his passion;
rather, by detaching it from external objects, he allows it to fill up his
inner being. This withdrawal from the world provides a kind of focus
and intensity to his spiritual life:

> He becomes solitary, and then he undertakes the movement . . .
> In the first place, the knight will then have the power to concen-
> trate the whole substance of his life into a single desire. If a
> person lacks this concentration, this focus, then he never manages
> to make the movement . . . In the next place, the knight will have
> the power to concentrate the conclusion of all his thinking into
> one act of consciousness. If he lacks this focus . . . he will never
> find the time to make the movement.[12]

The knight of resignation's passion draws together his scattered
attention, his various possibilities, and the push and pull of his
different habits and tendencies, and directs all of his energy towards
God. This gives unity, purpose and consistency to his life.

Through acceptance of his suffering, the knight of resignation
abandons those claims and expectations that make his relationship
to God conditional, as opposed to free. Genuine love is that which
expects no return (and as Kierkegaard remarks in his *Works of Love*,
love for someone deceased is for this very reason the purest, 'most
unselfish' kind of love[13]). The great cost of this movement, however,
is the happiness that may be gained from finite things, especially
from loving relationships with other people. Although resignation is
a 'monastic movement', most knights of resignation continue to live
in this world – but they are not at home here:

> Most people live completely absorbed in worldly joys and
> sorrows; they are benchwarmers who do not take part in the

dance. The knights of infinity are ballet dancers and possess elevation. They make the upward movement and come down again . . . but every time they come down, they are unable to assume the posture immediately, they waver for a moment, and this wavering shows that they are aliens in the world.[14]

For the knight of resignation, the fear inspired by existence – the constant threat of pain and loss symbolized by 'the sword hanging over the beloved's head' – remains incommensurable with the idea of God. Earthly happiness must be given up in order to gain the peace in the soul needed for religious love. There is some sense in which this contact with the eternal is suspended above worldly life: although the individual's love for God is passionate and real, the object of this love seems rather static, ideal, devoid of activity. For Johannes de silentio, 'that God is love' is a *thought* that comes and goes, and because it is merely ideal this thought has no power to change the finite world: 'to me God's love . . . is incommensurable with the whole of actuality'.

Although resignation uses up all of a person's strength, it still falls short of faith. Johannes de silentio recognizes that, although he is capable of resignation, he lacks the courage for faith. Abraham does not only give up what is most precious to him: he also remains confident that Isaac will somehow be restored to him. This is demonstrated by his calm assurance to his son that 'God will provide' something for the sacrifice. Resignation, a courageous act of will, brings Abraham to Mount Moriah, but his expectation that God will return Isaac to him is an act of faith: 'By faith Abraham did not renounce Isaac, but by faith Abraham received Isaac.'[15] Whilst the knight of resignation turns away from the world to focus on God, the 'knight of faith' returns to the world and lives within it happily, sustained by the belief that his life is blessed because it is a gift from God, and therefore a sign of His love. Abraham is 'higher' than the knight of resignation by virtue of his *descent*, his return to finitude, his movement back down to earth: 'Temporality, finitude – that is what it is all about.'[16] Johannes de silentio describes faith as a 'double movement': first the world is renounced, and then it is received back again. This 'double movement' is represented by Abraham's journey out to Mount Moriah, but then home again to his family life. It is also illustrated by the metaphor of the dancer, who descends gracefully to the ground after leaping into the air.

Kierkegaard's view that religious faith requires a leap has become one of his best-known ideas. A leap is a movement from one place, or one point, to another, and implies that these two points are different, unconnected – for if there were a path between them, it would be possible to walk the distance and there would be no need for a leap. Kierkegaard's concept of the leap is opposed to Hegel's theory of mediation, which represents precisely the 'path' that connects two positions and so overcomes the difference between them. One of Kierkegaard's examples of a leap is the transition from reflective thinking to existence, which involves 'a radical breach'.

Unlike mediation, the leap implies individuality: as the image of the dancer suggests, a leaping movement expresses the energy of a particular individual. Mediation, on the other hand, is an impersonal procedure of thinking, and although it requires some sort of effort it operates according to a rational principle that is indifferent to the existing individual. Whilst reason has a kind of necessity, the leap expresses freedom: 'the leap is . . . essentially at home in the realm of freedom'; 'the leap is the category of decision'; and 'all forms of instigation or impulsion constitute precisely an obstacle to making the leap in reality'.[17] Faith requires a leap because it holds together the contradictory opposites of eternity and temporality, infinity and finitude, God and the world. Whilst resignation responds to the disjunction between eternity and temporality by prioritizing the eternal, faith returns to the finite world. (In *Concluding Unscientific Postscript* Johannes Climacus suggests that 'leaping means to belong essentially to the earth and to respect the law of gravity, so that the leap is merely momentary'.[18]) The knight of faith believes, against reason, that the temporal world is a manifestation of God's eternal, unchanging love.

After renouncing his expectation of happiness in the movement of resignation, the knight of faith maintains a different sort of expectation. This is not based on the view that he has a right to happiness and justice, as if these are somehow due to him, but on the belief that God loves him like a father, caring about the smallest details of his life. This belief sustains an attitude of openness and receptivity, a readiness to receive a gift; whereas if we think that something is ours by right, then it can never be given to us as a gift. In order to accept his life as a gift from God, the knight of faith has to give up his expectations of gaining anything, but at the same time remain ready to gain *something*, without knowing what this will be. As soon as he receives his life from God, he has to give it up so that he can receive it once again. Both resignation and faith have to be repeated at every moment. This means that the movement of resignation is preserved within the leap of faith:

> Infinite resignation is the last stage before faith, so that anyone who has not made this movement does not have faith, for only in infinite resignation do I become conscious of my eternal validity [i.e. of my relationship to God], and only then can one speak of grasping existence by virtue of faith . . . Precisely because resignation is antecedent, faith is no aesthetic emotion but something far higher; it is not the spontaneous inclination of the heart, but the paradox of existence.[19]

Having accepted suffering through the movement of resignation, the knight of faith goes a stage further and accepts God's love also. This demands a different sort of courage, 'a paradoxical and humble courage', by virtue of 'the great mystery that it is far more difficult to receive than to give'.[20] It is difficult for the individual to receive God's love because the threat of suffering and loss remains, since it is integral to finite existence. Johannes de silentio admires above all the knight of faith: 'every moment to see the sword hanging over the beloved's head, and yet not to find rest in the pain of resignation but to find joy by virtue of the absurd – this is wonderful. The person who does this is great, the only great one'.[21]

The distinction between resignation and faith is similar to the distinction that is drawn in *Concluding Unscientific Postscript* between 'Religion A' and 'Religion B'. Resignation, like Religion A, is immanent: it is a matter of human effort. Speaking as a knight of resignation, Johannes de silentio emphasizes that 'I make this movement all by myself'.[22] This self-sufficiency marks the limitation of the movement of resignation. Faith, like Religion B, looks to God for something that the individual cannot gain by himself. Johannes de silentio says that 'he who loves God without faith reflects upon himself; he who loves God in faith reflects upon God'.[23] In a sense, the movements of resignation and faith go in opposite directions, of giving and receiving, although they are connected (a double movement, rather than two separate movements) insofar as giving makes receiving possible. Resignation gives away the finite world in order to give love to the eternal being; faith receives God's love, and in so doing also receives the finite world as His gift.

These parallels between resignation and faith, and Religions A and B, are rather surprising. Abraham is certainly not a Christian – but in the *Postscript* Religion B represents Christianity. This suggests that Kierkegaard's interpretation of the story of Abraham points towards Christianity, and illuminates the requirements of Christian faith. Both Abraham and the Christian are asked to believe in a self-contradictory God: Abraham's God contradicts Himself by promising to make Abraham the father of a nation, and then commanding him to kill his son; the Christian God contradicts Himself by becoming a human being. Abraham's situation is comparable to that of Jesus, for both men act in a way contrary to customary values, and find themselves excluded from society; both suffer in their relationship to God, and yet continue to have faith. Although *Fear and Trembling* does not discuss sin, it puts forward a view of the relationship between ethics and religion that fits in with the Christian doctrine of salvation. Because man is a sinner, he will always fall short of ethical righteousness and therefore cannot find salvation through the ethical, but must appeal to God's grace. This does not mean that ethics becomes redundant, but that salvation depends on something higher than the ethical, beyond the sphere of human justice.

ABRAHAM AND ETHICS – THREE PROBLEMS

Johannes de silentio considers three philosophical problems that arise from the story of Abraham: is there a teleological suspension of the ethical? Is there an absolute duty to God? Was it ethically defensible for Abraham to conceal his undertaking from Sarah and Isaac? The pseudonym's response to each of these questions leads to the conclusion that Abraham can be praised only if there is something higher than the ethical sphere. He begins his analysis of Problema I by stating that 'the ethical as such is the universal, and as the universal it applies to everyone [and] at all times'. Defining the ethical in terms of the universal echoes the theories of ethics offered by both Kant and Hegel: these philosophers view moral action as requiring the individual to act for the sake of the community as a whole. On this view, 'as soon as the single individual asserts himself in his singularity before the universal, he sins, and only by acknowledging this can he be reconciled again with the universal'. But if this really is the case, continues Johannes de silentio, then 'Hegel is wrong in speaking about faith; he is wrong in not protesting loudly and clearly against Abraham's enjoying honour and glory as a father of faith when he ought to be sent back to a lower court and shown up as a murderer'.[24]

Kierkegaard's point is that Abraham should be considered worthy of praise only if there can be a 'teleological suspension of the ethical'. The word 'teleological' comes from the Greek word *telos*, which means purpose or goal; in this context, suspending the ethical *teleologically* means putting it to one side for the sake of something else that lies outside the ethical sphere. This higher *telos* is, in fact, the single individual *as she stands in relationship to God*. From the point of view of ethics, the single individual has to subject herself to the universal, but if there is something higher than this then the individual can elevate herself above the universal by relating to the higher *telos*. What is interesting here is the fact that Kierkegaard is arguing not only that God is higher than the ethical, but that the individual's direct relationship to God (that is, her faith) is higher than the ethical too. He emphasizes that this idea is paradoxical and absurd:

> Faith is precisely the paradox that the single individual as the single individual is higher than the universal . . . This position cannot be mediated, for all mediation takes place only by virtue of the universal; it is and remains for all eternity a paradox, impervious to thought . . . [Abraham] acts by virtue of the absurd, for it is precisely the absurd that he as the single individual is higher than the universal. This paradox cannot be mediated . . .[25]

This view is very clearly directed against Hegel's philosophy, and in particular against his idea of mediation: for Hegel, the individual's relationship to God is mediated by her role within the community – the Christian's relationship to God, for example, is lived through her participation in a Christian community.

Kierkegaard clarifies the notion of a teleological suspension of the ethical by showing how Abraham is different from other mythical or historical figures who make the decision to kill their children. Euripides' character Agamemnon sacrifices his daughter Iphigenia to the gods, in exchange for a favourable wind that will ensure the success of his fleets in the Trojan war. In the Book of Judges,

Jephthah promises God that if He gives the Israelites victory in their battle with the Ammonites, he will offer as a sacrifice whatever comes from his house to meet him on his return from the battlefield; this turns out to be his only daughter, but Jephthah keeps his promise. Brutus, a Roman commander and politician, ordered that his son be executed for treason in accordance with the laws of the state. Kierkegaard puts Agamemnon, Jephthah and Brutus in the category of 'tragic heroes': they are tragic because they not only suffer the loss of their children, but actually take responsibility for this loss – and they become heroes because their actions save the nation, or at least uphold its laws. Their contemporaries understand their distress, and praise their great courage and honour. Tragic heroes do not require a teleological suspension of the ethical, because their actions remain within the ethical sphere: they give up one ethical duty for another, renouncing their family loyalty for the sake of their obligation to the community.

Abraham's situation is quite different. 'While the tragic hero is great because of his moral virtue, Abraham is great because of a purely personal virtue'. As well as transgressing his ethical duty to his family, he also jeopardizes the good of the community – because Isaac represents the future of the nation of Israel. There is no way that Abraham can be redeemed within the ethical; in fact, this kind of justification in the eyes of other people is precisely the temptation that he might give in to by disobeying God's command. 'Why, then, does Abraham do it? For God's sake and – the two are wholly identical – for his own sake. He does it for God's sake because God demands this proof of faith; he does it for his own sake so that he can prove it'.[26] Here again Kierkegaard claims that the individual's relationship to God, not just God Himself, stands over and above the ethical sphere.

Towards the end of the chapter on the teleological suspension of the ethical, Johannes de silentio points to a comparison between Abraham and Jesus. He suggests that, just as people tend to hear the story of Abraham but think little of his suffering or of the absurdity of his faith, so Christians can overlook these aspects of Jesus's life:

> Sweet sentimental longing leads us to the goal of our desire, to see Christ walking about in the promised land. We forget the anxiety, the distress, the paradox. Was it such a simple matter not to make a mistake? Was it not terrifying that this man walking

around amongst the others was God? Was it not terrifying to sit down to eat with him? Was it such an easy matter to become an apostle?[27]

This comparison implies that Jesus's own faith, and that of his disciples, also involves a teleological suspension of the ethical. Of course, Jesus did not attempt to kill anyone, nor ask anyone else to do so, but he still called into question the interpretation of the law and made it, in some cases, relative to an inward, more purely spiritual relationship to God. Jesus and his disciples often risked being misunderstood by their contemporaries, and they may not have been able to explain their faith in rational terms; Kierkegaard is certainly convinced that the notion that a human being could be divine is profoundly paradoxical. Johannes de silentio's conclusion applies equally to Abraham, to Jesus, and to authentic Christians: 'he who walks the narrow road of faith has no one to advise him – no one understands him. Faith is a marvel, and yet no human being is excluded from it; for that which unites all human life is passion, and faith is a passion'.[28]

The second Problema, 'Is there an absolute duty to God?', emphasizes once again that religious faith must be distinguished from the ethical sphere. Johannes de silentio remarks that people sometimes confuse the universal (that is, the ethical) with the absolute (that is, God), so that ethical duties become synonymous with the duty to God. On the contrary, argues the pseudonym,

> The paradox of faith . . . is . . . that the single individual is higher than the universal, that the single individual . . . determines his relation to the universal [the ethical] by his relation to the absolute [God], not his relation to the absolute by his relation to the universal. The paradox may be expressed in this way: that there is an absolute duty to God, for in this relationship of duty the single individual relates himself as the single individual absolutely to the absolute.[29]

This means that the ethical sphere is 'reduced to the relative', but Johannes de silentio is careful to point out that 'it does not follow that the ethical should be invalidated'. It is not easy to work out what exactly *should* happen to the ethical: we are told that it is not dismissed altogether, but suspended, relativized, or given 'a completely different expression' – but what does this mean in practice? Perhaps there will be no difference in the individual's outward behaviour, although inwardly she will be concerned with being true to God's will rather than with other people's judgements of her moral worth.

Again Johannes de silentio draws a comparison between Abraham's faith and Christianity, by citing a difficult passage from the gospel of Luke: 'If any one comes to me and does not hate his own father and mother and wife and children and brothers and sisters, yes, and even his own life, then he cannot be my disciple'. The pseudonym describes this as 'a remarkable teaching on the absolute duty to God'. His interpretation of Jesus's words suggests that, while they must be taken literally, they do not mean that the Christian expresses his love for God by becoming indifferent to those people dearest to him: on the contrary, the disciple's love for those he leaves behind testifies to the strength of his religious commitment. But why does Jesus talk about hatred? The pseudonym's response to this is not particularly clear, but he seems to be saying that the disciple will have to be prepared to act in a way that will make his family think that he hates them, even though he continues to love them whole-heartedly:

> The absolute duty can lead one to do what ethics would forbid, but it can never lead the knight of faith to stop loving. Abraham demonstrates this. In the moment he is about to sacrifice Isaac, the ethical expression for what he is doing is: he hates Isaac. But if he actually hates Isaac, then he can rest assured that God does not demand this of him . . . He must love Isaac with his whole soul. Since God claims Isaac, he must, if possible, love him even more, and only then can he *sacrifice* him, for it is indeed this love for Isaac that makes his act a sacrifice by its paradoxical contrast to his love for God. But the distress and the anxiety in the paradox is that he, humanly speaking, is thoroughly incapable of making himself understood.[30]

The knight of faith's inability to make himself understood is a recurring theme throughout *Fear and Trembling*, and Johannes de silentio focuses on this in Problema III, where he asks whether the fact that Abraham conceals his task of sacrificing Isaac can be justified in ethical terms. The short answer is no: the pseudonym argues that disclosure is essential within the ethical sphere, for it is this that allows a person's actions and intentions to be judged accurately. He contrasts this ethical requirement of openness with the more positive role of concealment within the aesthetic sphere, and then argues that Abraham's situation can be accommodated by neither ethics nor aesthetics.

From an aesthetic point of view, concealment is important, for the structure of a novel or a play is usually based on a dialectic of concealment and revelation. The plot develops around something that is at least partially hidden or unknown, and this creates a dramatic tension that is eventually resolved by the hidden element being brought into the open. Writers have at their disposal various dramatic devices – such as coincidences, intercepted letters, eavesdropping minor characters, and so on – which contrive to bring about this resolution. Johannes de silentio illustrates this point by returning to the example of Euripides' play *Iphigenia in Aulis*: Agamemnon remains silent about his decision to sacrifice Iphigenia, both because he is too heroic to seek comfort from another person, and because he wants to protect his family for as long as possible. On the other hand, the tears of his wife and daughter will add to the pathos of Agamemnon's fate and make him seem even more heroic. 'What does aesthetics do? It has a way out; it has the old servant in readiness to disclose everything'. This allows the integrity of Agamemnon's character to be maintained, while moving the story on and intensifying the drama.

But this cannot be translated into real life, which is the domain of ethics. Unlike aesthetics, 'ethics has no coincidence and no old servant at its disposal. The aesthetic idea contradicts itself as soon as it is to be implemented in actuality'. In the ethical sphere, it is up to the individual to disclose himself – to take responsibility for his actions and face the consequences. Although concealment might seem to make things easier for the other people involved, there is a danger that the real, perhaps sub-conscious, reason for keeping quiet is to make things easier for oneself. 'The tragic hero demonstrates his ethical courage' by disclosing his intentions: he exposes himself to the even greater suffering of seeing his loved ones' tears. However, the tragic hero gains from this self-disclosure a certain consolation – the consolation of being understood and admired by others, of being recognized as a hero. 'The relief provided by speaking is that it translates me into the universal . . . The tragic hero does not know the dreadful responsibility of loneliness'.[31]

Johannes de silentio argues that Abraham's silence is unacceptable to aesthetics, which requires the individual to be silent in order to protect someone else. This is not the reason for Abraham's silence; 'in fact, his whole task of sacrificing Isaac for his own and for God's sake is an offense to aesthetics, because it is able to understand that I sacrifice myself but not that I sacrifice someone else for my own sake'.[32] And of course, ethics cannot accommodate Abraham either, because it demands disclosure. In fact, Abraham *cannot* speak, because he knows that he will not be understood: he cannot explain himself to Sarah or to Isaac, because his actions do not make sense.

> Would not Sarah, would not Isaac say to him, 'Why do you want to do it, then? After all, you can abstain'. And if in his distress he wanted to unburden himself and clasp to himself all that he held dear before he proceeded to the end, the terrible consequence might be that Sarah and Isaac would take offense at him and believe him to be a hypocrite. Speak he cannot; he speaks no human language. And even if he understood all the languages of the world, even if those he loved also understood them, he still could not speak – he speaks in a divine language, he speaks in tongues.[33]

Abraham is sacrificing Isaac because he has faith in God, and this faith does not just mean that he loves God enough to give up what is most precious to him (this is resignation rather than faith), but that he believes that *God loves him* and will therefore remain true to His promise. Abraham has faith that 'it will not happen, or if it does, the Lord will give me a new Isaac, that is, by virtue of the absurd'. This belief is paradoxical, and cannot be justified.

Kierkegaard's interpretation of Abraham suggests that religious faith is so purely inward that it cannot be expressed through language. The religious person stands alone before God: she only has God to bear witness to her private suffering, and to console her for it. In living her life in relationship to God, she has to believe that God *does* love her and *will* provide consolation, since she has come to a place that cannot be shared with other human beings. However, as the example of Abraham shows, this faith involves holding on to finite things and continuing to love others – in fact, this earthly happiness is made sacred because it is treated as a gift from God, itself an expression of God's love. This is certainly a rather puzzling position – and of course, Kierkegaard would not want it any other way: he is intent on accentuating the paradoxical character of the religious life. Just as we conclude that his view of faith is too extremely solitary and individualistic, we find ourselves faced with his insistence that the religious person is uncompromising in her love for others. So then faith means living an ordinary life and being happy with it – and yet the knight of faith cannot hope to be understood by his friends and family.

Perhaps Kierkegaard is most concerned that faith should not be regarded as a worldly thing that is measured by the judgements of other people, and this is why he insists on its inwardness and incommunicability. His reference to the Sermon on the Mount, where Jesus says that one should keep one's religious observances private, supports this view. This means that Kierkegaard's individualism is a kind of by-product of his concern for authenticity, rather than the main focus of his account of faith – and he is careful to counter this by emphasizing the importance of loving others. It cannot be denied, however, that he is hostile to organized, institutional religion, and people who gain support and strength from belonging to a religious community may find this attitude difficult to accept. We might want to question whether Kierkegaard's sharp distinction between the ethical and religious spheres is completely and genuinely philosophical: he was temperamentally inclined to remain an outsider and an exception, and it seems that at times he did little to make himself better understood by his contemporaries. He saw himself mirrored in Abraham's situation, and maybe his interpretation of the story romanticizes his own inability to communicate – especially with Regine. On the other hand, his analysis of Abraham is philosophically compelling, and presents a powerful argument against the Hegelian view of religious faith.

CHAPTER 7

PHILOSOPHICAL FRAGMENTS: THE PARADOX OF CHRISTIANITY

SOCRATES, HEGEL AND CHRISTIANITY

Philosophical Fragments, which was published in 1844 under the pseudonym Johannes Climacus, focuses on the Christian doctrine of the incarnation: the appearance of God in the human form of Jesus of Nazareth. Throughout the text Climacus compares the perspective of philosophy, personified by Socrates, with the teaching of Christianity, and emphasizes repeatedly the profound difference between them. Whereas Socrates helped people to realize the truth which was in fact within them all along, Jesus (as the incarnation of God) actually gives a person something that she lacks, and could never acquire by herself. The truth that Jesus offers is not just wisdom, but salvation. This means that, in Christianity, the relationship between the teacher and the learner involves a fundamental change: the coming-into-existence of something that did not exist before.

This interpretation of the Christian incarnation challenges the Hegelian theologies and philosophies of religion that were so popular amongst many of Kierkegaard's contemporaries. Although Climacus uses the figure of Socrates to represent the non-Christian philosophical position, both Socrates and Hegel share the view that the truth is already latent within each individual, and must merely be 'recollected' in order to be known fully and explicitly. Hegel applies this understanding of truth to Christianity by regarding the incarnation as an historical event that manifests, or makes concrete, the eternal truth that the divine and human natures are unified. In other words, for Hegelians the purpose of the incarnation is to make explicit something that was already implicit. Climacus's concern to separate this 'Socratic' understanding of truth from Christianity is not supposed to be a criticism of Socrates (who died about four hundred years before Jesus was born). His intention is, rather, to oppose the Hegelian attempt to interpret Christianity according to a philosophical system based on this view of truth and knowledge.

Reading *Philosophical Fragments* would be much easier if the book began with an introduction explaining that its subject-matter is the incarnation, and that one of its main purposes is to challenge the Hegelian interpretation of Christianity. However, Johannes Climacus is very evasive about this basic orientation of the text. Although it soon becomes obvious that he is discussing the doctrine of the incarnation, he refers to it only in very abstract terms – in fact, he never uses the word 'incarnation', or the name 'Jesus's – and he does not mention Christianity until the last paragraph of the book. Likewise, although the text is full of allusions to Hegelian philosophy, in the form of remarks (usually contemptuous or sarcastic) about 'the system' and 'world-history', Hegel's name appears just twice, and both of these appearances are in footnotes rather than in the main body of the text. Only at the end of the final chapter does Climacus tell us that the book is, essentially, about 'the relation between Christianity and philosophy'.

Why is Climacus not explicit about the point of view of *Philosophical Fragments*? Why does he bother to mask his interest in Christianity, and his dissatisfaction with Hegelian philosophy, when these masks are so transparent? There are many possible answers to this question, and the reader may need to return to the discussion of Kierkegaard's methods of communication in Chapter 2 above. One of the interesting things about *Philosophical Fragments* is the way in which the pseudonym preserves a fine balance between neutrality and polemic, although it seems that his neutrality is a kind of mask that is actually in the service of the text's polemical intentions. (In other words, this neutrality is ironic.) In the 'Moral' at the end of the book, Climacus is careful to point out that he is contrasting the Socratic view with Christianity without claiming that one is more true than the other. Actually, Kierkegaard's polemic against Hegel does not require the pseudonym to express a preference for Christianity in opposition to the Socratic–Hegelian position: it is enough to show that these are really distinct, for this undermines Hegel's claim to have comprehended the truth of Christianity.

Because the end of the book illuminates its beginning, it is useful to consider its overall purpose before we examine the text in more detail. The title page of *Philosophical Fragments* includes, apart from the names of the 'author' Johannes Climacus and the 'editor' S. Kierkegaard, three questions: 'Can an historical point of departure be given for an eternal consciousness; how can such a point of departure be of more than historical interest; can an eternal happiness be built on historical knowledge?' It is relatively easy to see that these questions concern the relationship between history and eternity, but the significance of this relationship is not quite so clear – and indeed, it is not at all clear, especially to a modern reader, what is meant by 'an eternal consciousness'. The fact that these questions refer to the Christian teaching about salvation becomes explicit at the end of the book:

> As is well known, Christianity is the only historical phenomenon that despite the historical – indeed, precisely by means of the historical – has wanted to be the single individual's point of departure for his eternal consciousness, has wanted to interest him otherwise than merely historically, has wanted to base his happiness on his relation to something historical. No philosophy (for it is only for thought), no mythology (for it is only for the imagination), no historical knowledge (for it is only for memory) has ever had this idea – of which in this connection one can say, with all multiple meanings, that it did not arise in any human heart.[1]

In the pages between the initial questions and this eventual clarification of their Christian significance, Climacus argues that this connection between an historical event and each individual's personal salvation requires a philosophical understanding very different from that shared by Socrates, Hegel and most other philosophers. The pseudonym is particularly keen to emphasize that the truth of Christianity does not originate 'in any human heart', but must instead be given to each individual by God himself.

Another challenge that *Philosophical Fragments* presents is the fact that, as the title suggests, it offers fragments rather than a coherent system. This makes the text difficult to read and to understand, and even more difficult to summarize and explain. This, of course, is Kierkegaard's intention: he does not want simply to present a neatly packaged intellectual argument that can be compared and contrasted with other theories. His unwillingness to produce a system is itself part of his critique of Hegel and Hegelians, who were committed to systematic thinking. In dealing with the doctrine of the incarnation, the text is clearly engaging in theological as well as philosophical reflection, but Climacus's approach to the subject is quite different from conventional theology. Most of Kierkegaard's contemporaries assumed (and this view persists today) that the main task of theology is to integrate doctrinal claims into a rational framework, which will typically be based on a particular system of philosophy. However, there is no such framework to be found in *Philosophical Fragments*, although Climacus does offer a cluster of concepts that, when pieced together, provide a philosophy of the incarnation.

Even though this text does not have the rational, logical coherence and consistency that we expect of a conventional philosophical system, there is a single theme that is central to the book and links its different parts together. This theme is becoming, or 'coming into existence'. In the middle of the book, between chapters IV and V, there is an 'Interlude' in which Climacus discusses this idea of 'coming into existence'. This is, he suggests, the distinguishing feature of 'the historical': 'everything that has come into existence is *eo ipso* ["by this fact alone"] historical, for even if no further historical predicate can be applied to it, the crucial predicate of the historical can still be predicated – namely, that it has come into existence'.[2] Even nature is historical in this sense, but Climacus adds that in the case of free actions ? and here he seems to have in mind the actions of human beings, and also the actions of God – there is a double movement of 'coming into existence'. Climacus is referring here to choice and freedom. He says that this is 'the historical in the stricter sense', because here life contains 'a possibility of coming into existence within its own coming into existence'.[3]

Because Christianity is rooted in history, this movement of 'coming into existence' is central to the Christian notion of truth. From a Socratic point of view, the interaction between teacher and learner brings about the transition from ignorance to self-knowledge, whereas from a Christian point of view the transition is from sinfulness to salvation. (Climacus calls the state of sin 'untruth', and salvation – in other words, eternal life or eternal happiness – 'truth'. As we saw in Chapter 5, the pseudonym Anti-Climacus describes sin as a failure to be what one truly is, as a falling short of wholeness, and this illuminates the correlation between sin and 'untruth'.) The process of salvation is, suggests Climacus, like being born for a second time; it is a kind of 'coming into existence', because the individual becomes 'a *new* person'.[4] This movement of becoming is also present in the incarnation itself, when God enters history: here, says Climacus, 'the eternal' comes into existence, is actually born into the temporal, natural, historical world. As well as uniting the different aspects of the incarnation, the movement of 'coming into existence' also represents an implicit critique of Hegelian philosophy. We can recall from Chapter 3 that this issue of movement is central to Kierkegaard's attack on Hegel, for he complained that Hegelian philosophy could not accommodate the fact that existence means becoming – that existence is always, in fact, 'coming into existence'. For this reason, claiming that such a movement is essential to Christian teaching helps to set Christianity apart from Hegelian philosophy.

CLIMACUS'S PARADOX: HOW CAN TRUTH BE LEARNT?

Philosophical Fragments begins with a short, self-effacing preface that says nothing about the content of the book, although it covertly signals the author's opposition to Hegelian philosophy. The first chapter, entitled 'Thought-Project', introduces the philosophical perspective of Socrates by raising the question, 'can the truth be learnt?' This echoes a question that Socrates himself addressed, most famously in Plato's dialogue *Meno*, where he suggests that the idea of learning is paradoxical. The learner seeks the truth, and therefore does not already know it; but if he does not know it then he cannot seek it – for he does not know what he is looking for, and would be unable to recognize it even if he came across it. This has become a classical philosophical problem that is often known as 'Meno's Paradox'.

Socrates resolves this problem by suggesting that all learning and seeking are in fact a process of recollection. According to this view, truth is identified with eternal, unchanging Ideas or Forms, which exist separately from the temporal, historical world. We are able to gain access to this realm of truth because our souls are also eternal, and before joining with a particular body they were familiar with the Ideas or Forms. This means that our souls already possess knowledge, although it has been forgotten, and 'thus the ignorant person merely needs to be reminded in order, by himself, to call to mind what he knows'.[5] Johannes Climacus adds a footnote to his discussion of recollection, suggesting that 'this Greek idea is repeated in ancient and modern speculation'. In this context 'modern speculation' refers to Hegelian thought, and this indicates that what Climacus describes as 'the Socratic point of view' is supposed to represent Hegel's philosophy too. (At the end of his *Phenomenology of Spirit* Hegel himself draws attention to the similarities – and also the differences – between his own understanding of truth and knowledge, and the Socratic idea of recollection.)

Climacus explains that, from the Socratic point of view, the actual process of learning 'is something accidental, a vanishing point, an occasion'. The process of learning occurs in time, and is therefore historical, but this merely facilitates access to the eternal realm where the truth can be found. Climacus's point is that the truth already exists within the learner, and so the learner's interaction with the teacher is not essential to the truth itself. The teacher does not create the truth, or affect it in any way. In a sense it does not matter what the teacher says, or who the teacher is, or when the teaching takes place, for there are many different ways to encourage recollection and these all lead to the same truth. Socrates tended to prefer the method of questioning, for this made it clear that the student was discovering the truth within himself. As Climacus emphasizes, 'the ultimate idea in all questioning is that the person asked must himself possess the truth and acquire it by himself. The temporal point of departure is a nothing, because in the same moment I discover that I have known the truth from all eternity, without knowing it . . .'.[6]

Having outlined the Socratic model of truth, Climacus raises the question of how things would be if the learner did *not* already possess the truth. How, in this case, could the truth be learnt? The pseudonym suggests that 'if the situation is to be different [from the Socratic situation] then the moment in time must have such decisive significance that for no moment will I be able to forget it, neither in time nor in eternity, because the eternal, previously non-existent, came into existence in that moment'.[7] It soon becomes clear that this alternative situation represents the Christian view of the relationship between human beings and God. When Climacus uses the phrase 'the eternal', he is talking about truth: in the context of Greek philosophy, truth can be identified with the realm of eternal Forms, whereas in the context of Christianity truth signifies salvation or eternal life. In the Socratic relationship the individual already possesses the truth, and the teacher has the role of the midwife; in the Christian relationship the individual in her natural condition lacks the truth. In the Socratic situation, the truth is made explicit; in the Christian situation, the truth is brought into existence. If the truth actually comes into existence, then the moment when this occurs has 'decisive significance', because it contains a profound transformation.

Although Climacus presents the idea that the individual lacks the truth, or 'is in untruth', as an abstract hypothesis, this is in fact the Christian presupposition of sin – which we encountered in *The Concept of Anxiety* as the dogmatic claim that we are all sinners. Climacus emphasizes that the individual is responsible for her state of untruth: 'this state – to be untruth and to be that through one's own fault – what can we call it? Let us call it *sin*'.[8] Even though sinfulness tends to include a resistance to recognizing and acknowledging that one is a sinner, the individual can become aware of this with the help of someone else. Here 'recollection' is possible, and the relationship between teacher and learner is Socratic, because the individual is discovering something that already exists within herself. But the further movement of acquiring the truth – the movement from sinfulness to salvation – cannot happen Socratically, because in this case something entirely new must be brought into existence. In fact, because the truth is absolutely different from the individual's present state, she will not be able to comprehend it. This means that whoever gives the truth must also give the individual the ability to understand or receive it – and this ability or 'condition', Climacus later reveals, is faith:

> Now, if the learner is to obtain the truth, the teacher must bring it to him, but not only that. Along with it, he must provide him with the condition for understanding it, for if the learner were himself the condition for understanding the truth, then he merely needs to recollect . . . But the one who not only gives the learner the truth but provides the condition is not a teacher. Ultimately, all instruction depends upon the presence of the condition; if it is lacking, then the teacher is capable of nothing, because . . . the teacher, before beginning to teach, must transform, not reform, the learner. But no human being is capable of doing this; if it is to take place, it must be done by the god himself.[9]

From a theological point of view this is very important. Although faith is a person's subjective response to God, Climacus is claiming that we are not even capable of this by ourselves. Faith, as well as salvation, is a gift from God. Throughout Kierkegaard's thought there is an interesting tension between this idea, and the seemingly contradictory claim that faith, like sin, comes from the human will. Perhaps the best way to understand this is to regard the tension as something positive that should be maintained within the individual's religious life. Believing that faith lies beyond one's own power emphasizes one's dependence on God, and encourages an attitude of gratitude and humility. On the other hand, it is also important to maintain a sense of responsibility for one's life, to keep up a regular practice of prayer, and to make an effort to respond to God in the right way. (This combination of receptivity and effort is important within other religious traditions, not just Christianity.)

Climacus presents the alternative to the Socratic situation in terms of Christian categories, although he does not actually discuss the doctrine of the incarnation. The state of untruth is called *sin*; the condition for receiving the truth is called *faith*; the god who gives both the truth and its condition is a *saviour*, a *deliverer*, a *reconciler* and a *judge*; the transformation in the individual is called *conversion*, *repentance* and *rebirth*; the moment in which this transformation occurs is called *the fullness of time* (see Paul's Letter to the Galatians, 4.4). As I have suggested, this Christian model of truth is distinguished from the Socratic model by the concept of 'coming into existence', for this is what gives the moment 'decisive significance'.

> In *the moment*, a person becomes aware that he was born, for his previous state, to which he is not to appeal, was indeed one of 'not to be'. In *the moment*, he becomes aware of the rebirth, for his previous state was indeed one of 'not to be'. If his previous state had been one of 'to be', then under no circumstances would the moment have acquired decisive significance for him. Whereas the Greek pathos focuses on recollection, the pathos of our project focuses on the moment, and no wonder, for is it not an exceedingly pathos-filled moment to come into existence from the state of 'not to be'?[10]

It is important to bear in mind that 'the moment' is not something that occurs just once, as if at a certain point in time the individual's life is transformed from an enduring state of sinfulness to an enduring state of faith, repentance, truthfulness and so on. Instead, the moment must be continually repeated, for as we saw in Chapter 5 the individual's relationship to God has to be constantly renewed. Existence is *always* becoming, and it is *always* dependent on God, so if it is not becoming truthfully – in faith and repentance – then it is becoming sinfully. For this reason, Climacus emphasizes that 'the moment' has such decisive significance 'that for no moment will I be able to forget it'. According to this view, the Christian's ordinary day-to-day life is charged with the continual presence of eternity.

In chapter II of *Philosophical Fragments*, Climacus explores further the role of 'The God as Teacher and Saviour'. Why, he asks, does God want to appear before the learner? God cannot be moved by need – for He lacks nothing – and therefore He must be moved by love. Climacus suggests that the love-relationship between God and the human individual is destined to be unhappy, because it is unequal, 'and only in equality and in unity is there understanding'. As Climacus makes clear in the following chapter, the inequality of the relationship is due to the human condition of sin. This is such a profound difference between God and man that there is a problem of communication between them: man is unable to understand God, and this will make God unhappy, just as a lover will suffer if her beloved is unable to understand her.

> The unhappiness is the result not of the lovers being unable to have each other but of their being unable to understand each other. And this sorrow is infinitely deeper than the sorrow of which people speak, for this unhappiness aims at the heart of love and wounds for eternity . . . This infinitely deeper sorrow is identified essentially with the superior person, for he alone also understands the misunderstanding.[11]

Having raised this issue, Climacus offers an analogy to the situation between God and man by telling the story of a king who loves a poor, ordinary girl. Because the king is sensitive, and genuinely in love, he worries that the girl would be unhappy in such an unequal relationship, and so he wishes to bring about equality between them. He can do this either by raising the status of the girl, or by lowering himself to her level. If he chooses the first option, though, the girl's equality with him would be an illusion, since it would be brought about by the king's power: even if she thinks she is equal, he knows otherwise, and so his love will still be unhappy. This means that the union between the lovers must be brought about by the king's descent: he must become as lowly as the person whom he loves.

If we apply this story to the relationship between God and man, then God, who wishes to communicate with even the very lowest person, must become this person's equal. Of course, 'the lowliest of all is one who must serve others – consequently, the god will appear in the form of a *servant*'. This is not merely a disguise, but a genuine transformation, and in becoming a lowly servant God risks the contempt of other people, who do not understand that he is also God: 'the form of the servant was not something put on. Therefore the god must suffer all things, endure all things, be tried in all things, hunger in the desert, thirst in his agonies, be forsaken in death, absolutely the equal of the lowliest of human beings'.[12] Climacus emphasizes that this suffering demonstrates the depth and power of God's love: in the form of a servant, God lives a life of 'sheer love and sheer sorrow'.

Love is an important theme in *Philosophical Fragments*, particularly in this chapter on 'The God as Teacher and Saviour' and in the following chapter on 'The Absolute Paradox'. Climacus suggests an intimate connection between love and understanding: love seeks to be understood by the beloved, but also human understanding resembles a lover insofar as it seeks contact with something beyond itself. We will examine this idea in more detail in a moment, but if we take a step back from this section of *Philosophical Fragments* we can gain a sense of its significance within the context of Kierkegaard's thought as a whole. As we have seen in earlier chapters, Kierkegaard wishes to show that philosophy and faith are concerned with fundamentally different forms of truth: the truth as knowledge, and the truth as love. He regards his pseudonymous authorship as 'a polemic against the truth as knowledge' that attempts to outline an alternative, religious notion of truth, which is a task not merely for the individual's intellect, but for her whole being and especially her heart. In *Fear and Trembling* Abraham is portrayed as a model of this kind of truth, truthfulness or faith: 'what did Abraham achieve? He remained true to his love'. Johannes Climacus's discussion of the incarnation continues this 'polemic against the truth as knowledge' by suggesting that the understanding can relate passionately to something that is beyond its reach. Even though this 'something' *cannot be known*, there is nevertheless a certain kind of truth that happens in this encounter.

In chapter III of *Philosophical Fragments*, Climacus introduces the notion of paradox. First he mentions Socrates, who was aware of a certain contradiction within himself: he 'was not quite clear . . . whether he was a more curious monster than Typhon or a friendlier and simpler being, by nature sharing something divine'. To be both these things at once seems paradoxical, says Climacus,

> But one must not think ill of the paradox, for the paradox is the passion of thought, and the thinker without the paradox is like the lover without passion: a mediocre fellow. But the ultimate potentiation of every passion is always to will its own downfall, and so it is also the ultimate passion of the understanding to will the collision, although in one way or another the collision must become its downfall. This, then, is the ultimate paradox of thought: to want to discover something that thought itself cannot think. This passion of thought is fundamentally present everywhere in thought, also in the single individual's thought insofar as he, thinking, is not merely himself.[13]

Thought is inclined to reach further and further beyond itself, taking what is not yet understood and making it transparent, ordered and intelligible. This is how knowledge grows. By this tendency, however, the understanding will eventually come into contact with something that is not merely unknown but *unknowable*, unintelligible – and this is the paradox. Climacus's suggestion that this movement of thought is passionate is very striking, since many philosophers have made a strong distinction between reason and passion. These are both elements of human nature, but the pursuit of wisdom is usually regarded as the task of reason alone: emotions or passions are unruly and likely to lead us astray, and so they need to be kept in check by reason. To claim that the understanding, which is the faculty of reason, is itself passionate subverts this opposition between reason and passion.

The understanding, in inclining towards the unknown, 'wills its own downfall'. This is not a conscious attempt at self-destruction, but rather the inevitable outcome of the desire to increase and deepen wisdom. The understanding moves in the direction of the paradox 'without really understanding itself'. Because the paradox is precisely the unknown, it is difficult for Climacus to tell us what it is – for this is something that simply cannot be explained. However, in talking about the relationship between the understanding and the paradox, he is clearly trying to express a view of man's relationship to God:

> What is this unknown against which the understanding in its paradoxical passion collides and which even disturbs man and his self-knowledge? It is the unknown. But it is not a human being, insofar as he knows man, or anything else that he knows. Therefore, let us call this unknown *the god*. It is only a name we give to it.[14]

Climacus is careful to say that 'God' is just a name he gives to 'the unknown', because there is a danger that, in discussing the unknown and trying to say what it is, the understanding may project concepts onto it, and so confuse itself with it. We might want to say that God is the unknown, and that the incarnation is a paradox because a single individual is at once divine and fully human, at once infinite and finite, at once eternal and mortal. In fact, to say that Jesus was fully human is to suggest that he understood the experience of being a sinner, and yet as the incarnation of God he must surely have been completely pure – and this seems completely contradictory. But even though we can recognize that a paradox *is* a paradox, our attempts to describe it give it a certain content that actually comes from ourselves, from within our understanding, which contains only that which it is possible for us to think. God is absolutely different, and we cannot conceive of this difference without compromising it, without making it into something accessible to us: 'in defining the unknown as the different the understanding ultimately goes astray and confuses the difference with likeness'. Despite the understanding's best efforts to assimilate the unknown, it simply cannot be grasped. God is 'the absolutely different in which there is no distinguishing mark. Defined as the absolutely different, it seems to be on the point of being disclosed, but not so, because the understanding cannot even think the absolutely different . . . this difference cannot be grasped securely'.[15] It is important to note that this does not mean that rational thought has no role to play in the individual's relationship to God. On the contrary, reason, in pursuing knowledge, drives itself towards the paradox and even seeks it out. In this sense reason is 'passionate'.

Climacus criticizes attempts to demonstrate the existence of God, because these make the mistake of assuming that the unknown is accessible to reason. Many philosophers and theologians have produced arguments that claim to prove that God exists, and even though these are very numerous they can be grouped into just three or four main types of argument. Although Climacus addresses specific arguments, he also suggests that any attempt to demonstrate God's existence is nonsensical. If God does not in fact exist, then of course it is impossible to prove that He does. Even if God does exist, this existence cannot 'emerge' from the demonstration, because as long as one is in the process of proving it the conclusion has not yet been reached. The existence is there only 'when I let go of the demonstration', and this 'letting go', says Climacus, 'is a *leap*'. His point is that between the argument and its conclusion there is a gap in which something new comes into existence: the demonstration does not lead smoothly to the existence of God. Whether or not we agree with Climacus's analysis – or can even make sense of it – we can recognize that he is trying to highlight a disjunction, a lack of continuity, between thought and existence. This reinforces his insistence that we cannot gain access to God through reason. There seems to be a connection between letting go of a rational argument and the downfall of the understanding in its encounter with God.

Climacus's discussion of the paradox is especially difficult. This is partly because it deals with something unthinkable: in reading chapter III of *Philosophical Fragments* we find ourselves experiencing precisely what he describes: a desire to assimilate what is beyond our reach, to make sense of what is unintelligible. There is another difficulty, however, insofar as there are two variations of the paradox, which Climacus does not distinguish clearly. These are both forms of interaction between the human and the divine: on the one hand, there is the encounter between the individual and God, and on the other hand, there is the incarnation, in which God and man are one and the same being. (Climacus is more explicit about this version of the paradox in *Concluding Unscientific Postscript*, where he states, 'that God has existed in human form, has been born, grown up, and so forth, is . . . the Absolute Paradox'.[16]) The 'absolute difference' between man and God is sin, and in both of these cases this difference is somehow overcome, *without the difference being compromised*. Christianity is paradoxical 'by bringing into prominence the absolute difference of sin and by wanting to annul this absolute difference in the absolute equality'.[17] As we have seen, Anti-Climacus echoes this interpretation of Christianity in *The Sickness Unto Death*: 'it seems to be working against itself by establishing sin so securely as a position that now it seems utterly impossible to eliminate it again – and then it is this same Christianity that by means of the Atonement wants to eliminate sin as completely as if it were drowned in the sea'.

Although the understanding falters and submits itself when it collides with the paradox, it is not destroyed by this encounter: 'it is not annihilated but is taken captive . . . it can come to life again'. Reason can reassert itself against the paradox and continue to collide and struggle with it. 'If the paradox and the understanding meet in the mutual understanding of their difference, then the encounter is a happy one, like love's understanding' – but this happy relationship is not established securely. It endures only if the understanding continually steps aside. Just as sin continually becomes new and so continually requires repentance, just as Abraham's faith is renewed in every step towards Mount Moriah, so reason must repeatedly defer to the paradox if the individual is to maintain a relationship to God. This relationship is never fixed, but always 'coming into existence'.

There is always the possibility that reason will assert itself against the paradox, instead of surrendering itself in order to allow a happy relationship to take place. In this case the understanding will refuse to accept the paradox, and will simply judge it to be 'foolishness'. Climacus describes this hostile reaction as 'offense', and discusses it in an appendix to chapter III. He suggests that offense is like an 'acoustical illusion', a sound that seems to be coming from one place but actually comes from somewhere else. It seems that, in the encounter between the paradox and the understanding, it is the understanding that finds the paradox to be foolish and absurd. However, in fact it is the other way around: the paradox exposes the foolishness and absurdity of the understanding in trying to reach beyond itself and pass judgement on what is completely different and therefore unknowable. 'The offense remains outside the paradox', but still it attempts to express an opinion about it. So, in colliding with the paradox the understanding has two alternatives: it can accept its limitations and step aside, or it can foolishly assert itself and push the paradox away.

Kierkegaard's claim in this text and elsewhere that Christianity is paradoxical is clearly directed against Hegelian philosophy.

Whereas Hegel and his followers explain Christian doctrine in conceptual terms, and claim that reason can penetrate to the very heart of God's essence, Kierkegaard argues that the truth of Christianity is inaccessible to reason. Whereas Hegelian thought unites or mediates opposites, Kierkegaard insists that opposites cannot be reconciled – or, perhaps more accurately, he insists that this reconciliation cannot be understood. In *Concluding Unscientific Postscript* Climacus claims that the absolute paradox 'is the opposite of mediation'. From the human perspective it is impossible to overcome the absolute difference that is due to sin, and in Kierkegaard's view attempting to do this is just a deepening of sin because it refuses to acknowledge man's complete dependence on God. In this respect, he thinks that Hegel and Hegelians have missed the point of Christianity.

FAITH AND HISTORY

Chapters IV and V of *Philosophical Fragments* focus on the situation of the learner, follower or disciple of the divine teacher. Here Climacus continues to emphasize that God not only provides the learner with the truth, but with the condition for understanding it. In fact, the truth in this case *is* the paradox of the incarnation, and so it is not a question of understanding the paradox, but rather of 'coming to an understanding' with it. This involves recognizing that the paradox *is* a paradox, and accepting it anyway. The condition for this 'understanding' is faith:

> How, then, does the learner come to an understanding with the paradox, for we do not say that he is supposed to understand the paradox but is only to understand that this is the paradox . . . This occurs when the understanding and the paradox happily encounter each other in the moment, when the understanding steps aside and the paradox gives itself, and the third something, the something in which this occurs . . . is that happy passion to which we shall now give a name . . . we shall call it *faith*. This passion, then, must be that above-mentioned condition that the paradox provides. Let us not forget this: if the paradox does not provide the condition, then the learner is in possession of it; but if he is in possession of the condition, then he is *eo ipso* himself the truth, and the moment is only the moment of occasion.[18]

As Climacus has already pointed out in chapter I, the fact that both the truth *and* the condition for receiving it cannot be acquired by the individual alone distinguishes this situation from the Socratic relationship between teacher and learner. In this case, the teacher and the teaching – in other words, the incarnation – are one and the same thing, and this also means that the source of faith is also the object of faith. God gives the individual faith, which is the ability to see that He *is* God, even though He looks like any other human being. This is thoroughly paradoxical: 'in order for the teacher to be able to give the condition, he must be the god, and in order to put the learner in possession of it, he must be man. This contradiction is in turn the object of faith and is the paradox, the moment'.[19]

Because the learner is absolutely dependent on the teacher, 'faith must constantly cling firmly to the teacher'. This ongoing need for God is really at the very heart of the text, because it highlights the difference between the pagan and the Christian understanding of the human condition. From the Socratic point of view, every individual has access to the truth; from the Christian point of view, every individual is a sinner. Climacus makes this contrast more clear by describing the state of sin as 'untruth', which produces a straightforward distinction between truth and untruth. The attitude of Socrates' student will be very different from the attitude of the Christian disciple:

> The person who understands Socrates best understands specifically that he owes Socrates nothing, which is what Socrates prefers, and to be able to prefer this is beautiful . . . But if the whole structure is not Socratic – and this is what we are assuming – then the follower owes the teacher *everything* (which one cannot possibly owe to Socrates, since, after all, as he himself says, he was not capable of *giving birth*).[20]

This dependence on God, and the fact that the historical, incarnate God is both the source and the object of faith, seems to suggest that those who were contemporary with Jesus had a great advantage over those who chose to follow him after his death. Climacus takes care to show that this is not the case. Because Jesus's divine nature was not evident in his physical appearance – after all, he had to be fully human in order to be able to communicate with other human beings – it was no more immediately accessible to his contemporaries that to later generations of believers. The fact that Jesus was God can only be an object for faith, not for sense-perception, and this means that the contemporary disciple was in essentially the same situation as Christians are today.

In chapter IV, 'The Contemporary Follower', Climacus argues that 'immediate contemporaneity can only be the occasion' for any kind of knowledge. It can be the occasion for the individual to acquire historical knowledge; or to deepen his knowledge of himself according to the Socratic model; or to receive faith from God and witness a divine revelation. Living at the same time as Jesus is not the condition for receiving the truth, but an occasion for receiving both the condition and the truth – those who come later will have a different occasion, but they will receive the condition and the truth in the same way. The contemporary follower 'is not an eyewitness (in the sense of immediacy), but as a believer he is contemporary in the *autopsy* of faith. But in this autopsy every non-contemporary (in the sense of immediacy) is a contemporary'. Climacus's use of the word 'autopsy' here is striking: literally, this means 'the personal act of seeing', and the pseudonym is suggesting that every disciple is con-temporary with her own relationship to God. He regards the incar-nation as a living reality: whether it is in the present or the past it remains a paradox, and this paradox *is* the truth and 'the moment' of Christianity in which faith comes into existence. Climacus adds that the contemporary of Jesus is more fortunate than later follow-ers only because the years that elapsed after the historical life of Jesus allowed time for 'a great deal of chatter amongst men about this thing'. Even at the time there were 'untrue and confused rumours' about Jesus, and as these developed and increased over the centuries the right relationship to the incarnation became obscured. No doubt Kierkegaard intends to include Hegelian interpretations of Christianity amongst these 'untrue and confused rumours', for he thought that these were not only misguided but actually damaging to the 'task of becoming a Christian', since they led people in the wrong direction.

The fifth and final chapter of *Philosophical Fragments* focuses on the situation of 'The Follower at Second Hand', and here Climacus considers first the generation that came immediately after Jesus's contemporaries, and then the very latest generation of the 1840s. Because the earlier disciples were closer historically to the 'jolt' caused by the event of the incarnation, they lived with greater awareness of it – but this awareness can lead to faith or to offense, and so their proximity to the event did not itself bring them into a right relationship to God. Climacus observes that by the nineteenth century faith has been 'naturalised', woven into the fabric of European society and culture, and so become more normal, accept-able, and familiar. He does not consider this to be a good thing, because it encourages people to believe that they are Christians as a matter of course, as if one were simply 'born into' Christianity. In fact, says Climacus, 'to be born with faith is just as plausible as to be born twenty-four years old'.

However, Climacus's main point in this chapter is that, just as there is no essential difference between Jesus's contemporaries and all subsequent generations, there is no essential difference between the earlier and later of these non-contemporary generations. In each case the historical situation of the individual is merely an occasion, and does not affect the way she relates to God. Of course, these his-torical situations are themselves different: for Jesus's contemporaries the occasion for faith is their first-hand experience, whereas for sub-sequent generations the reports of contemporaries – which are the basis for the New Testament scriptures – provide the occasion for faith. This means that even though all Christians owe everything to God, later Christians also owe something (in the merely Socratic sense) to the people who recorded the events of Jesus's life and death:

> The contemporary's report is the occasion for the one who comes later, just as immediate contemporaneity is the occasion for the contemporary . . . There is no follower at second hand. The first and latest generations are essentially alike, except that the latter generation has the occasion in the report of the contemporary generation, whereas the contemporary generation has the occa-sion in its immediate contemporaneity and therefore owes no generation anything.[21]

It is significant that Climacus does not even mention the Church here, because although we would not expect him to regard a human institution as *decisive* for faith, it seems that nevertheless it provides the *occasion* for many people to become Christians. This refusal to allow the Church any role in assisting the individual's relationship to God reflects Kierkegaard's negative attitude towards to the Danish Church in general.

Between chapters IV and V there is an 'Interlude', which Climacus likens to a piece of music that is played between two acts of a play, to indicate an interval of several years. He suggests that, after the divine teacher has lived, died and been buried, 'precisely eighteen hundred and forty-three years have passed', and this of course is the period of time between Jesus's historical life and the writing of *Philosophical Fragments*. The 'Interlude' raises the question, 'Is the past more necessary than the future?' and addresses this question with a rather technical philosophical discussion of freedom and necessity, and possibility and actuality. Possibility and actuality are categories that were first introduced into philosophy by Aristotle, who made them central to his explanation of change and becoming. As we have seen, Kierkegaard was very interested in becoming, and he often makes use of Aristotle's categories of possibility and actuality when he wishes to show that the movement of 'coming into existence' is essential to 'the task of becoming a Christian'.

In this 'Interlude' Climacus's main point is that everything that comes into existence – and this includes the whole of history – does so freely; he argues that the past is *not* more necessary than the future. Here he is opposing Hegelian philosophy, which regards historical processes as reflecting a kind of logic that allows us to understand them rationally. According to this view, we can look back through history and see that particular events were inevitable, or necessary, developments of what had happened previously. Against Hegel, Climacus argues that everything historical has come into existence, and that 'no coming into existence is necessary – not before it came into existence . . . and not after it came into existence . . . All coming into existence occurs in freedom, not by way of necessity'.[22] The movement of coming into existence is not, he claims, something that can be perceived directly: we can perceive that something is present, or that something is absent, but we cannot perceive the process of becoming itself. This means that the historical is not the object of knowledge, but of belief:

> The historical cannot become the object of sense perception or of immediate cognition, because the historical has in itself the very illusiveness that is the illusiveness of coming into existence . . . belief believes what it does not see; it does not believe that the star exists, for that it sees, but it believes that the star has come into

existence. The same is true of an event. The occurrence can be known immediately, but not that it has occurred, not even that it is in the process of occurring, even though it is taking place, as they say, right in front of one's nose.[23]

Applying this principle to the incarnation, Climacus suggests that belief, or faith (the Danish word *Tro* can be translated as either belief or faith) is the only way to respond to it, since it was an historical event. More than this, however, it was not an ordinary historical event, but a 'self-contradiction' because it united the absolutely-different natures of God and man. This means that it requires two 'levels' of faith: faith in what cannot be perceived, as in the case of any historical fact, and faith in what cannot be understood, because this particular fact 'has a unique quality' – it is paradoxical.

Climacus's focus on 'coming into existence' in the 'Interlude' is, as I suggested at the beginning of this chapter, the key to this text, at least from a philosophical point of view. It represents the movement from untruth to truth – from sinfulness to forgiveness – that is the Christian notion of salvation. It represents the event of the incarnation, when God Himself comes into existence, becomes an historical fact. Both of these instances of 'coming into existence' present alternatives to the Socratic view of the human condition, and to the Socratic understanding of the divine (which here is synonymous with truth) as simply eternal and separate from history. More importantly, this undermines the Hegelian understanding of history in general, and of Christianity in particular. Climacus argues in the 'Interlude' that coming into existence cannot be immediately perceived, and must be the object of belief rather than knowledge. His insistence that both the incarnation and the individual's relationship to it are absolutely paradoxical emphasizes that in this case belief is not just dealing with uncertainty, but with a complete failure of the understanding. This opposes the claim of Hegelian philosophers and theologians that the truth of Christianity can be understood and explained by means of concepts.

Whereas Hegel offers an interpretation of Christianity that reflects his philosophical system as a whole, *Philosophical Fragments* suggests that this Hegelian system is basically Socratic, and argues that Christianity requires a radically different understanding of truth. In the 'Moral' at the very end of the book Climacus claims that the Socratic and the Christian positions are so different that it is not possible to say that one is more true than the other, since each has its own criteria of truth:

> This project indisputably goes beyond the Socratic, as is apparent at every point. Whether it is therefore more true than the Socratic is an altogether different question, one that cannot be decided in the same breath, inasmuch as a new organ has been assumed here: faith; and a new presupposition: the consciousness of sin; and a new decision: the moment; and a new teacher: the god in time.[24]

This claim defies any Hegelian attempt to reconcile or mediate the two positions. Here Climacus sets out the elements that distinguish the situation of the Christian 'learner' from the situation of the Socratic 'learner', and this makes it quite clear that the Socratic view of how truth is acquired – or more generally the philosophical, rational method – cannot be applied to Christianity.

CONCLUSION

Kierkegaard's insistence that philosophical concepts cannot do justice to the meaning of Christianity does not lead him to dismiss philosophy altogether, but, on the contrary, to expand it. Philosophers have traditionally understood truth as a relationship between ideas and reality, and Kierkegaard's account of subjective truth follows this model. However, instead of saying that truth happens when ideas and reality correspond to one another, he suggests that subjective truth requires ideas to be *realized*, turned into reality. The ideas that most interest Kierkegaard are ideas about the future: they are possible ways of being or courses of action, which are turned into reality by being chosen, and kept real by repeating this choice continually. Because life is always in motion, truth is itself a process of becoming.

This philosophical account of truth blends with Kierkegaard's analysis of religious faith: Abraham is the father of faith because he *remained true to his love*. Faith is the opposite of sin, which is a continual lapse away from God and into 'untruth'. In this way Kierkegaard brings together a philosophical notion of truth and a theological notion of salvation. Although he argues that philosophy and faith belong to different spheres of existence, he nevertheless produces a philosophy of the religious life. Of course, this philosophy itself belongs to the aesthetic sphere: it presents a possibility that will not become real unless it is accepted, committed to, and lived out day by day.

Kierkegaard's books call for a personal response on behalf of the reader – a willingness to turn inwards, to discover truths about herself, to make choices, to become a more authentic human being. To respond to Kierkegaard is to respond to one's own condition, and in particular to take responsibility for one's life. At the same time, however, we are told that this involves recognizing our limitations, our propensity to make mistakes, and our need for forgiveness. I cannot say too much about this personal kind of response, because it is up to you whether or not to accept Kierkegaard's interpretation of truth – and if so, to decide what, or who, you are going to be true *to*.

Of course, Kierkegaard's work also calls for a philosophical response: for analysis, judgement and evaluation of his position. The peculiar style in which he presents his ideas makes it hard to know how to go about this, especially if the reader is already trained in more conventional techniques of philosophical analysis. As we have seen, Kierkegaard does not attempt to construct a rational system or offer a series of logical arguments in support of his position. In fact, it might be difficult to test the validity and value of Kierkegaard's claims *without* relating them to one's own existence. But, from a more objective point of view, we can evaluate the coherence and consistency of his thought, and when we do so we find that his attempt to combine apparently disparate elements of philosophy, theology, psychology and personal experience is remarkably effective. Each text presents a unified, cohesive argument, and so does his authorship as a whole. Kierkegaard's claim that subjectivity is truth; his insistence on the dynamic quality of human life; his exposure of the gap between knowledge and existence; and his distinction between aesthetic, ethical and religious forms of life, recur throughout the authorship and give his thought continuity and consistency.

On the other hand, there are certainly elements within Kierkegaard's thought that appear to be in tension with one another. For example, there is some conflict between the ethical and religious approaches to life: the ethical person is strong, decisive and responsible for herself, and she maintains her authenticity through a continuous act of will, whereas the religious person has to let go of this wilfulness and become receptive to something beyond herself. In a way the religious sphere seems simply to contradict the ethical sphere. However, it also makes sense to claim that only after doing her very best to be ethical can the individual recognize that she is unable to overcome her sinful condition through her own efforts, and, choosing faith rather than despair, accept her limitations with humility and humour. For Kierkegaard, tension, conflict and

contradiction are positive forces that can lead to spiritual growth –
this is why he criticizes Hegel for trying to resolve them. He regards
Hegel's philosophy of mediation as symptomatic of a widespread
attitude of complacency that tries to avoid the more difficult aspects
of existence and is unwilling to explore the depths of the human
soul. Considering oneself to be a Christian might, in this case, be an
obstacle to genuine religiousness, since it allows no space for growth.

But does Kierkegaard, in seeking to correct this attitude, make
Christianity *too* difficult? Are his standards of authenticity unrea-
sonably high? Kierkegaard seems to think that it is essential to consider oneself incapable of being a Christian, and for this very reason
in need of God's help – because acknowledging this need is precisely
the essence of Christianity. Paradoxically, Christianity is possible
only if it is recognized as impossible. Kierkegaard's accentuation of
the paradoxical character of faith is unusual within the Christian
tradition, but it is consistent with the orthodox teaching that human
sinfulness means that people inevitably fall short of their ideals. This
self-understanding is likely to have a negative effect if taking responsibility for sin gets mixed up with notions of blame, guilt and punishment, but Kierkegaard tends to focus on more positive responses
to sin, such as forgiveness, repentance and faith.

Kierkegaard's philosophy is shaped by his concern to clarify the
meaning of Christianity, and his analysis of human existence draws
on specifically Christian concepts. In *The Point of View for My Work
as An Author* he insists that his entire authorship is an attempt to
communicate to readers the truth about Christianity. But what can
we gain from reading Kierkegaard if we are not ourselves engaged
in the task of becoming a Christian? Can Kierkegaard's interpretation of faith be applied to other religious traditions? And can his
philosophy offer anything to people who have a non-religious
outlook? Because he discusses religious questions from the perspective of the existing individual, rather than beginning with dogmatic
theological claims, some of Kierkegaard's ideas can illuminate other
forms of religious life – after all, issues like faith, love, suffering and
freedom are important within most traditions.

It is possible to extract from Kierkegaard's writings a purely philosophical account of the human condition. Indeed, philosophers
such as Martin Heidegger and Jean-Paul Sartre have done precisely
this, and the 'existentialist' philosophy they developed had an enormous impact on the intellectual and artistic culture of the twentieth

century. Like Kierkegaard, Heidegger makes the perspective of the existing individual central to his thought: in his influential book *Being and Time* he presents a meticulous analysis of the human way of being in the world, which makes use of Kierkegaard's notions of authenticity, movement and repetition. Although Heidegger excludes God from his philosophy, his later, increasingly spiritual writing echoes Kierkegaard's emphasis on receptivity to something beyond the self.

Sartre is even more determinedly atheistic than Heidegger, but he draws heavily on Kierkegaard's account of human freedom. Rather like Judge William in *Either/Or*, Sartre insists that people have to make choices and commitments, and take responsibility for their lives; however, being influenced by Marx as much as by Kierkegaard, he presents this as a political, even revolutionary act. But it is interesting that this radical, subversive, and certainly irreligious kind of existentialism is rooted in ideas that reflect Kierkegaard's concern to make people *more* authentically Christian. In eliminating the Christian aspects of Kierkegaard's thought, existentialists like Heidegger and Sartre tend also to pay less attention to themes such as love and suffering, which come so naturally to a Christian thinker. Of course, love and suffering are universal human experiences, and Kierkegaard's commitment to exploring them makes his philosophy unusually tender and affecting.

For some readers (and for others who refuse to read Kierkegaard at all) the personal elements within his philosophy, together with his polemical style and his refusal to submit himself to a rational system, mean that he is not a 'proper philosopher'. But one of the most basic philosophical problems is the relationship between ideas and existence, and the fact that Kierkegaard includes his own existence in his response to this problem only deepens and enriches it. Isn't it surprising that this approach seems to be so original? In fact, Kierkegaard's willingness to bring his personal life into his philosophizing is a reaction against the increasing professionalism of philosophy. He saw that, whereas Socrates had engaged in a passionate pursuit of wisdom, driven by a concern for the salvation of his soul, modern philosophy had become dry, lifeless and too worldly. Perhaps this is a caricature, and probably Kierkegaard was unfair to Hegel and his followers, but his deeply spiritual philosophy is still a timely reminder that love (*philo*) and wisdom (*sophia*) go together.

Although Kierkegaard emphasizes the difficulty of communication, he has managed to communicate to generations of readers his profound and original vision of the human condition. One of the joys of reading Kierkegaard's books is the opportunity to enter into an intimate relationship with the author: his distinctive, passionate and troublesome voice shines through the various pseudonyms and offers a glimpse into his inner world. More than any other works of philosophy, Kierkegaard's texts communicate from one subjectivity to another, from one existing individual to another. The way in which he brings his own life – including its prejudices and its anxieties – into his writing encourages the reader to be moved by the ideas she finds there.

FURTHER READING

Kierkegaard's Life and Works

Jane Chamberlain and Jonathan Rée (eds), *The Kierkegaard Reader*, Blackwell, 2001.

Joachim Garff, *Søren Kierkegaard: A Biography*, Princeton University Press, 2005.

Alastair Hannay, *Kierkegaard: A Biography*, Cambridge University Press, 2001.

Kierkegaard, *Journals and Papers* (seven volumes), Indiana University Press, 1967–78.

Kierkegaard, *Papers and Journals: A Selection*, Penguin, 1996.

Bruce Kirmmse (ed.), *Encounters With Kierkegaard*, Princeton University Press, 1996.

Walter Lowrie, *Kierkegaard*, Oxford University Press, 1938.

Josiah Thompson, *Kierkegaard*, London: Gollancz, 1974.

The Question of Communication

Kierkegaard, *The Point of View for My Work as an Author*, Princeton University Press, 1998.

Louis Mackey, *Kierkegaard: A Kind of Poet*, University of Pennsylvania Press, 1971.

George Pattison (ed.), *Kierkegaard on Art and Communication*, Macmillan, 1992.

Roger Poole, *Kierkegaard: The Indirect Communication*, University of Virginia Press, 1993.

Kierkegaard's Critique of Hegel

Clare Carlisle, *Kierkegaard's Philosophy of Becoming: Movements and Positions*, State University of New York Press, 2005.

Kierkegaard, *Either/Or*, Princeton University Press, 1987.

Tom Rockmore, *Before and After Hegel: An Historical Introduction to Hegel's Thought*, Hackett, 2003.

Jon Stewart, *Kierkegaard's Relation to Hegel Reconsidered*, Cambridge University Press, 2003.

Mark C. Taylor, *Journeys to Selfhood: Hegel and Kierkegaard*, Fordham University Press, 2000.

Subjectivity and Truth
C. Stephen Evans, *Kierkegaard's Fragments and Postscript*, Humanity Books, 1999.
Kierkegaard, *Concluding Unscientific Postscript*, Princeton University Press, 1992.
Jonathan Lear, *Therapeutic Action: An Earnest Plea For Irony*, Other Press, 2004.
Ed Mooney, *Selves in Discord and Resolve*, Routledge, 1996.
George Pattison, *Kierkegaard: The Aesthetic and the Religious*, SCM Press, 1999.
Merold Westphal, *Becoming a Self*, Purdue, 1996.

The Problem of Sin
C. Stephen Evans, *Søren Kierkegaard's Christian Psychology*, Regent College Publishing, 1995.
David Gouwens, *Kierkegaard as a Religious Thinker*, Cambridge University Press, 1996.
Kierkegaard, *The Concept of Anxiety*, Princeton University Press, 1981.
Kierkegaard, *The Sickness Unto Death*, Princeton University Press, 1980.
Sylvia Walsh, *Living Christianly: Kierkegaard's Dialectic of Christian Existence*, Penn State Press, 2005

Kierkegaard's Fear and Trembling
Kierkegaard, *Fear and Trembling*, Princeton University Press, 1983.
John Lippitt, *Kierkegaard's Fear and Trembling*, Routledge, 2003.
Ed Mooney, *Knights of Faith and Resignation*, State University of New York Press, 1991.
Anthony Rudd, *Kierkegaard and the Limits of the Ethical*, Oxford University Press, 1997.

Kierkegaard's Philosophical Fragments
Stephen M. Emmanuel, *Kierkegaard and the Concept of Revelation*, State University of New York Press, 1995.
C. Stephen Evans, *Passionate Reason*, Indiana University Press, 1992.
Kierkegaard, *Philosophical Fragments*, Princeton University Press, 1985.

Other topics
M. Jamie Ferreira, *Love's Grateful Striving*, Oxford University Press, 2001.
Amy Laura Hall, *Kierkegaard and the Treachery of Love*, Cambridge University Press, 2002.
Alastair Hannay, *Kierkegaard and Philosophy: Selected Essays*, Routledge, 2003.
Celine Leon, *Feminist Interpretations of Søren Kierkegaard*, Penn State Press, 1997.

Stephen Mulhall, *Inheritance and Originality: Wittgenstein, Heidegger, Kierkegaard*, Oxford University Press, 2003.

George Pattison, *Kierkegaard's Upbuilding Discourses*, Routledge, 2002.

Jolita Pons, *Stealing a Gift: Kierkegaard's Pseudonyms and the Bible*, Fordham University Press, 2004.

Mike Weston, *Kierkegaard and Modern Continental Philosophy: An Introduction*, Routledge, 1994.

Merold Westphal, *Kierkegaard's Critique of Religion and Society*, Penn State Press, 1991.

REFERENCES

Unless otherwise stated, all references are to volumes in the series *Kierkegaard's Writings*, published by Princeton University Press and translated by Howard V. Hong and Edna H. Hong (with the exception of *The Concept of Anxiety*, which is translated by Reidar Thomte and Albert Anderson).

CHAPTER 1

1 *The Point of View for My Work as an Author*, p. 80
2 *The Point of View for My Work as an Author*, p. 80
3 *Journals and Papers* 5430
4 Bruce Kirmmse, *Encounters With Kierkegaard*, pp. 229–30

CHAPTER 2

1 *Concluding Unscientific Postscript*, pp. 248–9
2 *The Point of View for My Work as an Author*, p. 45
3 *Journals and Papers* 6433
4 *Repetition*, p. 131

CHAPTER 3

1 *Journals and Papers* 1608
2 *Either/Or* volume 2, p. 176
3 *Either/Or* volume 2, p. 173
4 *Either/Or* volume 2, p. 171
5 *Either/Or* volume 2, p. 171
6 *Either/Or* volume 1, p. 39
7 *Either/Or* volume 1, p. 26

CHAPTER 4

1 *Concluding Unscientific Postscript*, p. 50
2 *Journals and Papers* 2809
3 *Concluding Unscientific Postscript*, p. 197
4 *Concluding Unscientific Postscript*, p. 203
5 *Concluding Unscientific Postscript*, p. 195
6 *Repetition*, p. 149
7 *Concluding Unscientific Postscript*, pp. 213–5
8 *Concluding Unscientific Postscript*, pp. 324–7

CHAPTER 5

1 *Journals and Papers* 1032
2 *Journals and Papers* 7602
3 *The Concept of Anxiety*, p. 58 (note)
4 *The Concept of Anxiety*, pp. 31, 33 (note), 35
5 *The Concept of Anxiety*, p. 61
6 *The Concept of Anxiety*, p. 154
7 *The Concept of Anxiety*, pp. 154, 159
8 *The Sickness Unto Death*, pp. 13–14
9 *The Sickness Unto Death*, p. 23
10 *The Sickness Unto Death*, p. 82
11 *The Sickness Unto Death*, p. 71
12 *The Sickness Unto Death*, p. 73
13 *The Sickness Unto Death*, p. 94
14 *The Sickness Unto Death*, pp. 105, 130
15 *The Sickness Unto Death*, p. 100
16 *The Sickness Unto Death*, p. 14

CHAPTER 6

1 *Journals and Papers* 6491
2 *Fear and Trembling*, p. 3
3 *Fear and Trembling*, p. 7
4 *Fear and Trembling*, p. 33
5 *Fear and Trembling*, p. 38
6 *Fear and Trembling*, pp. 10–11
7 *Fear and Trembling*, p. 14
8 *Fear and Trembling*, pp. 19–21
9 *Fear and Trembling*, p. 48
10 *Fear and Trembling*, p. 44
11 *Fear and Trembling*, p. 50
12 *Fear and Trembling*, p. 42
13 *Works of Love*, p. 349
14 *Fear and Trembling*, p. 41

15 *Fear and Trembling*, p. 49
16 *Fear and Trembling*, p. 49
17 *Journals and Papers* 2352; *Concluding Unscientific Postscript*, pp. 109, 199
18 *Concluding Unscientific Postscript*, p. 124
19 *Fear and Trembling*, pp. 46–7
20 *Fear and Trembling*, p. 104
21 *Fear and Trembling*, p. 50
22 *Fear and Trembling*, p. 48
23 *Fear and Trembling*, p. 37
24 *Fear and Trembling*, pp. 54–5
25 *Fear and Trembling*, pp. 55–6
26 *Fear and Trembling*, pp. 59–60
27 *Fear and Trembling*, p. 66
28 *Fear and Trembling*, p. 67
29 *Fear and Trembling*, p. 70
30 *Fear and Trembling*, p. 74
31 *Fear and Trembling*, pp. 113–14
32 *Fear and Trembling*, p. 112
33 *Fear and Trembling*, p. 114

CHAPTER 7

1 *Philosophical Fragments*, p. 109
2 *Philosophical Fragments*, p. 75
3 *Philosophical Fragments*, p. 76
4 *Philosophical Fragments*, p. 18
5 *Philosophical Fragments*, p. 9
6 *Philosophical Fragments*, p. 13
7 *Philosophical Fragments*, p. 13
8 *Philosophical Fragments*, p. 15
9 *Philosophical Fragments*, p. 15
10 *Philosophical Fragments*, p. 21
11 *Philosophical Fragments*, pp. 25–6
12 *Philosophical Fragments*, pp. 32–3
13 *Philosophical Fragments*, p. 37
14 *Philosophical Fragments*, p. 39
15 *Philosophical Fragments*, pp. 44–6
16 *Concluding Unscientific Postscript*, p. 217
17 *Philosophical Fragments*, p. 47
18 *Philosophical Fragments*, p. 59
19 *Philosophical Fragments*, p. 62
20 *Philosophical Fragments*, 61
21 *Philosophical Fragments*, pp. 104–5
22 *Philosophical Fragments*, p. 75
23 *Philosophical Fragments*, pp. 81–2
24 *Philosophical Fragments*, p. 111

INDEX

Abraham 20, 21, 32, 41, **110–17**, 141, 145, 153
Adam 92, 95, 96–9, 109
aesthetic sphere, aesthetic individual 11, 22, 30, 56–61, 75, **77–9**, 82–9, 112–13, 129–30, 153
Agamemnon 125
Anti-Climacus 35–6, 101–8, 145
anxiety 97–101
Aristotle 42, 50–1, 53, 56, 57, 79
atonement 100, 107, 145
Augustine, St 93, 95, 97
authenticity 71–2, 116

becoming 21, 40–1, 71–3, 94, 107, 108, 116, 135–6, 140, 150 *see also* change
Bible 31
Brøchner, Hans 8
Brutus 126
Buddha, Buddhism 29, 87

change 21, 73 *see also* becoming
childhood, Kierkegaard's 6–7, 17
choice 56–60, 98 *see also* freedom
Christendom 70
Christianity 7, 20, 25–6, 31–2, 51, 63–74, 76, 80–1, 91–4, 107, 116–17, 124, 128, 132–53
Climacus, Johannes 26–8, 32, 35–6, 63–70, 75, 78, 80–1, 122, 132–52

communication 18, **25–44**, 157
concealment 129–30
Concept of Anxiety, The 90, **94–101**, 138
Concluding Unscientific Postscript 13, 23, 26–8, 33, 60, **63–75**, 78, 80–2, 122–3, 144, 146
Constantin Constantius 72–3
contradiction 50, 53, 55–6, 60
Corsair, The 13, 20

death, Kierkegaard's 14
defiance 104–5
Descartes, René 48, 62
desire 98
despair 78–9, 101–8

Edifying Discourses 2, 3, 13, 85
Either/Or 11–12, 18–19, 22–3, 26, 30–1, 34, 36, 40, 44, 55, **56–62**, 75, 77–8, 95–6, 112
either/or 53–61
ethical sphere, ethical individual 11, 57–61, 68, 71, 75, **78–80**, 82–9, 116–17, 124–31
empiricism 71
Enlightenment 48–9
'essential knowledge' 66
existentialism 155–6
existing individual 15, 25–6, 37, 43–4, 57, 62, 72, 76, 122

faith 20–1, 41, 61, 74–6, 80–1, 92, 100, 102–4, 107–8, 111–31,

138–41, 146–52 *see also* fidelity
Fear and Trembling 12, 21, 32, 48, 100, **110–31**, 141
fidelity 71–3, 116
forgiveness 80, 92–3, 95, 108
freedom 11, 18–19, 26, 38, 43, 57–60, 74, 78, 79, 84–5, 94, 98–9, 150

gift 122–4, 130, 139 *see also* grace
God 18, 20, 22, 25, 48, 51, 53–5, 68, 71, 80, 86, 91–3, 96, 98–9, 101–3, 105–9, 114–30, 136–46
grace 80, 108–9, 124 *see also* gift

happiness 19, 81, 119, 122, 130
Haufniensis, Vigilius *see Concept of Anxiety*
Heiberg, Johan 52–5
Heidegger, Martin 5, 155–6
Hegel, G.W.F. 3–4, 17, 42, **45–62**, 66, 70, 72, 86, 88, 111–14, 118, 122, 124–5, 132–7, 155
honesty 71, 116
humour 83

Incarnation, doctrine of 60–1, 74, 80–1, 132–48, 151
indirect communication 3, **25–32**
individual *see* existing individual
individualism 17–18, 88, 131
inwardness 22–3, 28, 62, 68, 71, 74, 78, 84, 86, 88, 131
irony 81–3, 85–6

Jephthah 126
Jesus 29, 51, 53, 61, 66, 68, 74, 80, 82, 99, 100, 116, 124, 126–8, 131–2, 143, 147–9
Johannes de silentio 110–30
journals, Kierkegaard's 14, 23–4
Judaism 51, 53–4, 91
Judge William 56–60

Kant, Immanuel 49, 62, 79, 118, 124

Kierkegaard, Michael 6–8
knight of faith, knight of resignation *see* faith, resignation
knowledge *see* essential knowledge, objective knowledge, subjective knowledge

leap, leap of faith 41, 86, 118, **122**, 123, 144
logic (Hegelian, Aristotelian) 50–5
love 96, 116–17, 120–3, 128, 130, 140–1, 156
Luther, Martin 93, 95, 97

Martensen, Hans 52–5, 56, 70
mediation 50–61, 72, 86, 112, 122, 125, 146, 155
metaphor 40–1
Mill, John Stuart 79
moment, the 139–40, 152
Moment, The 14
movement 42–3, 59, 116, 136 *see also* becoming
Mynster, Bishop 53–7

necessity (logical) 39, 150
Nietzsche, Friedrich 5, 22, 86–7
nihilism 21–2, 78, 88

objective knowledge, objective truth, objectivity 27, 65, 67–70, 73, 88–9, 116, 141–2

paradox 61, 74, 80–1, 113–14, 123, 125–7, 131, 136, 142–7
passion 22, 68, 73–4, 113–15, 120, 127, 142–3
Paul, St 88
Philosophical Fragments 60, 63, 74, 132–52
philosophy
  Kierkegaard's attitude to 15–17, 32, 35, 37, 39–44, 56, 58, 61–2, 153, 156
  Kierkegaard's study of 8, 48

Plato 73, 136

Point of View for My Work as an Author, The 14, 17, 155

possibility, possibilities 67, 77, 78, 84–5, 98–9

principle of contradiction 50 *see also* contradiction

pseudonyms 23, 28, 32, **33–9**

rational thought 15, 32, 41–2, 142–6

rationalism 48–52

reality 49–52, 78

reason *see* rational thought

receptivity 29, 31, 81, 85, 122–4, 139

recollection 73, 132, 136–9

reflection 17, 60, 75, 112–13

Regine Olsen 9–11, 14, 19, 21, 24, 72, 131

religion A and B 80–1, 123–4

religious discourses *see* Edifying Discourses

religious sphere, religious individual 75, **80–1**, 83–9 *see also* faith

repentance 92, 96, 107, 140

Repetition 12, 19, 36–7, 40–3, 72–3

repetition 35, 43, 72–3, 79, 116, 123, 140, 145

resignation 119–24

responsibility 10, 19, 57, 79, 95, 138–9

resurrection 74

Romanticism 77

salvation 66–7, 80, 124, 132–8, 151, 153

Sartre, Jean-Paul 5, 155–6

seducer 77–8

self 101–2

Sibbern, F.C. 52–3

Sickness Unto Death, The 90, **101–9**, 145

sin 80–1, **90–109**, 124, 135, 138–40, 144–7

Socrates 16, 26–7, 38, 80, 82, 105, 132–8, 142, 147, 156

spheres of existence 61, **75–89**

style (Kierkegaard's writing) 12, 26, 40–3, 47–8, 56

subjective knowledge 27, 38

subjectivity 62, **63–89**

suffering 19–21, 100–5, 117–24

teacher (religious) 75–6, 137–41, 146–7

teleological suspension of the ethical 125–7

tragic heroes 126, 129 *see also* Agamemnon, Brutus, Jephthah

Trinity, doctrine of 51, 53

truth 21, 25–9, 51–2, 55, **63–89**, 114, 116–17, 132–42, 153

Works of Love 120